the **impati** embroiderer

the **impatient** embroiderer

jayne emerson

PHOTOGRAPHS BY **JOHN HESELTINE**

POTTER
CRAFT

New York

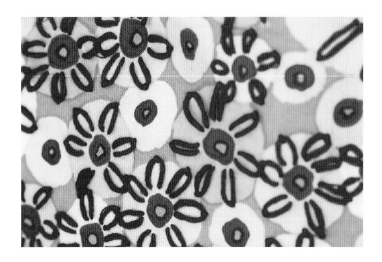

Copyright © 2006 Coats Crafts UK
Text and design copyright © 2006 by Jayne Emerson

All rights reserved.
Published in the United States by Potter Craft, an imprint of
the Crown Publishing Group, a division of Random House,
Inc., New York.
www.crownpublishing.com
www.clarksonpotter.com

Originally published in Great Britain by Coats Crafts UK,
in 2006.

Potter Craft and Clarkson N. Potter are trademarks,
and Potter and colophon are registered trademarks of
Random House, Inc.

Library of Congress Cataloging-in-Publication Data is
available upon request.

ISBN 0-307-33657-3

Printed in Singapore

Project editor and stylist Susan Berry
Editor Sally Harding
Designer Anne Wilson
Photographer John Heseltine

10 9 8 7 6 5 4 3 2 1

First American Edition

contents

introduction

When I tell people that I am an embroiderer, they usually ask me where I find the patience. They conjure up a vision of me painstakingly hand embroidering complicated cross-stitch designs or huge samplers. I believe that this misconception about what embroidery is, or can be, prevents many people from exploring the beauty, simplicity, and sheer fun of using machine and hand stitches for decoration.

The stores are full of embroidered garments and accessories these days. Much of it is exciting and surprisingly easy to make at home. It is just a matter of picking up an embroidery needle or mastering the hidden possibilities of your sewing machine. The intricate detail of antique embroideries is captivating, but the truth is that although I appreciate and collect samples of the most beautiful work, I rarely spend more than a couple of hours completing a stitching project of my own.

Modern embroidery, particularly in fashion and interiors, now focuses on experimentation with and exploitation of time-honored techniques and on finding new ways to create and use fabrics and textures. These fresh ideas have inspired my designs for this book. On the following pages you will find, among other contemporary stitching textures, appliqué with frayed, raw edges, hand embroidery on printed fabrics, and machine embroidery using thick threads—old techniques imbued with bold, up-to-date effects.

Most of my designs use machine embroidery, and a few incorporate simple hand embroidery, but I created them all with the impatient embroiderer in mind. You will see that through careful choice of fabrics, colors, and threads, you can produce beautiful effects with very simple hand and machine stitches. Essential, easy-to-master techniques are explained in full in "Basic Skills" (see pages 14–29). Be sure to read all the tips for machine embroidery. You may be surprised to find that even the most basic sewing machine has the capacity to effortlessly and beautifully decorate and embellish fabric.

The projects in this book are varied. I hope when you see how easy yet lovely they are, you will be inspired to make up your own designs as well. If you prefer textured effects, then experiment using a single color palette so that the stitches will stand out. You can achieve interesting texture with masses of small machine-embroidered stitches or just a few bold hand-embroidered stitches in thick thread. If creating successful color combinations is your goal, then consider whether you would like embroidery with the vibrant impact of starkly contrasting colors or a much softer, gentler effect with colors that blend together. Through trial and error, you will quickly discover which colors and textures you prefer.

For even quicker results, try using the embroidery designs and simple techniques in this book to decorate your own readymade garments or home furnishings. This will surely inspire you to start from scratch.

fabrics and threads

Although in the past most embroidery was worked on plain (often cream-colored) linen, canvas, or silk, we now live in an age when many traditional design rules are being broken. This presents us with a great opportunity to experiment in a whole range of ways.

It is fun to play with new grounds for embroidery, and I love stitching on patterned fabric, using the print motifs as a starting point for the stitch ideas (see the little purses on pages 70 and 72, for example). Printed fabric motifs also make interesting contemporary appliqué (see the doilies on pages 86 and 88). You can even take embroidery further and create a whole new textured textile by stitching several layers of fabric together and then cutting slits into the layers (see the hot water bottle cover on page 100). Or try making a lace fabric by working swirling, overlapping machine stitches on water-soluble vanishing fabric (see the bowls on pages 90–95).

When you add the relatively new inventions of water-soluble fabric and fabric adhesive spray into the mix of the wide range of fabrics and threads available, there are endless possibilities for embroidery designs.

Inspiration for embroidery designs can be found everywhere; the colors in your garden or on a postcard can be perfect starting points. Keep in mind, however, that although poppies sprinkled in an ocher field look gorgeous, the color combination works because the ocher is only dotted with red: proportions are what make a color scheme work.

I often find I spend more time choosing color and print combinations than I do on the actual embroidery. Limiting fabrics in this book to Rowan's patchwork collection (see pages 108 and 109) and using just a few types of thread encouraged me to narrow my palette and focus more on texture and form when creating the designs. A good way to learn how to mix colors is to look carefully at a fabric print you are drawn to and analyze the palette. You will then be able to use a similar color combination for an embroidery design of your own.

As far as the fabrics for embroidery are concerned, cotton is a good choice, and I have used it for all my designs here. It cuts easily and does not slip underneath the needle when sewn. It is also durable, can sustain frequent washing, and

is nice to the touch. If you make any of my embroideries in another kind of fabric, the look will be quite different. I hope that if you are new to embroidery, you will move on to explore the many possibilities of silk, wool, and textured cloths and threads. Some of the projects in this book could be transformed completely if worked in, say, tweed or embroidered with a metallic yarn.

As far as technical ability is concerned, the whole point of needlecraft is to create a lovingly stitched item, so never mind if the lines go a little wobbly at times. If embroidery is too pristine, it can end up looking store-bought or industrially produced. Embroidery need not be complex to create an impact. No matter how small the embroidery or how little time it took you, it will always be appreciated and treasured.

I won't pretend that this book is a comprehensive guide to embroidery, because it is not. What it delivers is a thorough introduction to some basic hand- and machine-embroidery techniques.

I used the Rowan collection of patchwork fabrics for this book, in part so you can copy the projects exactly if you wish. However, there is a wonderful range of fabrics out there from other sources (including thrift shop bargains), so do not be deterred from experimenting with whatever you can find.

The matte quality of cotton embroidery thread works well with my designs, but there are many beautiful specialist embroidery threads on the market, and I urge you to experiment with these—just be careful not to let their beauty distract from your design. Mixing fibers can produce interesting results. Remember, there are no restrictions for modern embroidery.

Right: Samples of some of the embroidery techniques used in this book: hand embroidery on a floral print (top), machine-embroidered lines created with thick cotton embroidery thread (center), raw-edge appliqué stitched to the ground fabric with free-motion machine embroidery (bottom).

equipment

Even though the embroidery designs in this book are very simple, for satisfying results it is important to make them well, with a professional finish. Since they are quick and easy to stitch, you can concentrate on doing a good job.

The list on this page covers the equipment required for various tasks. Many of the items you will probably be able to find in your general-purpose sewing box. Also, you will not need all of the equipment recommended here for every project in the book.

Choose sewing threads with care. Most fine threads will work for basting. For permanent seams and hems, if you are working with natural cottons as recommended, use natural cotton sewing thread. Always use sewing thread that is slightly darker than the fabric, as a lighter thread might stand out garishly along the seams.

When embroidering by hand or machine, make sure you work in good light. Natural daylight is best, but if this is not possible, daylight bulbs can provide a good alternative.

The rotary cutting equipment that is used for patchwork is handy for cutting strips, rectangles, and squares of fabric. You might not want to purchase this equipment for your projects if you are a beginner embroiderer, but it is worth considering adding it to your equipment if you get hooked on the craft.

For preparing appliqué templates
Pencil for tracing and drawing templates
Tracing paper for tracing template shapes
Stiff, thin cardboard for templates
Pair of sharp scissors or craft knife for cutting paper and cardboard

For marking fabric
Tailor's chalk pencil or water-soluble pen or pencil
Dressmaker's carbon paper

Special preparation aids
Water-soluble vanishing fabric
Fusible bonding web (paper-backed web of adhesive)
Fabric adhesive spray for temporary basting
Water-soluble vanishing thread for basting (optional)

For cutting fabric
Iron and ironing board for preparing fabric for cutting
Tape measure and ruler
Pair of sharp dressmaker's shears
Pinking shears (optional)
Rotary cutter, rotary-cutter mat, and ruler (all optional)
Paper for making paper pattern pieces—graph or plain

For hand stitching and hand embroidery
Small pair of embroidery scissors
Stainless steel pins
Selection of sewing needles—"sharps" for hand sewing hems and basting; crewel embroidery needles for hand embroidery; beading needle for small beads
Thimble
Embroidery hoop

For machine stitching and machine embroidery
Good sewing machine with basic attachments—including general-purpose foot, darning foot, and zipper foot
Supply of sewing machine needles—medium-size needles (80/12) for machine embroidery
Embroidery hoop for free-motion machine embroidery

Threads
Fine cotton sewing threads for basting, seams, and fine machine embroidery
Six-stranded cotton embroidery floss for hand embroidery
Thick cotton sewing thread for bold machine embroidery

Right: Here is the key equipment, except for a sewing machine, iron, and ironing board, needed for simple machine and hand embroidery. Make sure you have this equipment at hand before starting a project.

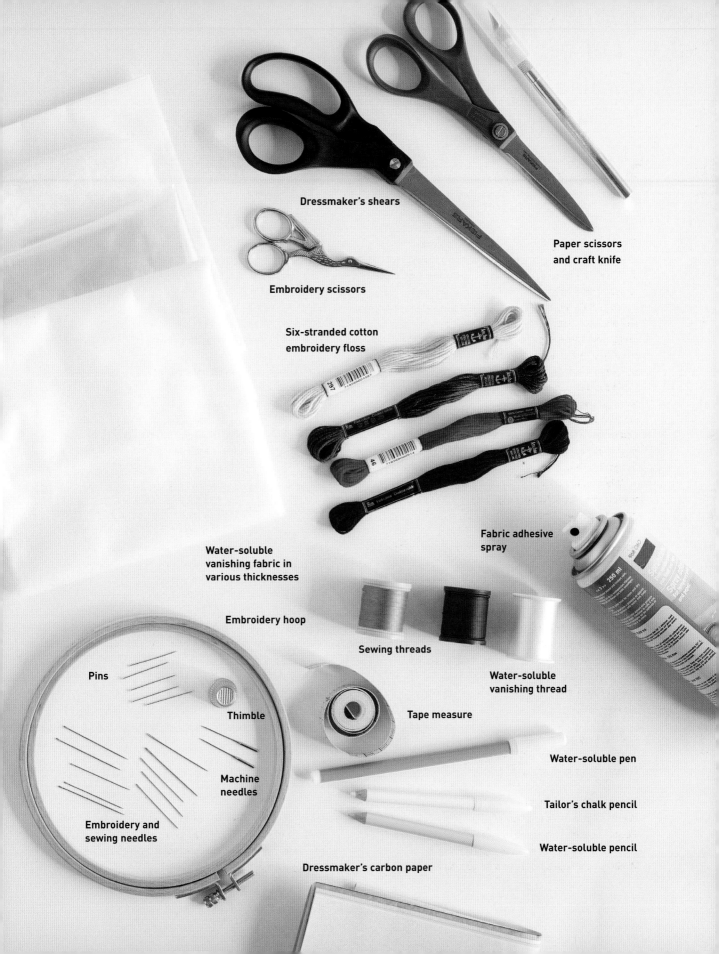

Dressmaker's shears

Paper scissors
and craft knife

Embroidery scissors

Six-stranded cotton
embroidery floss

Fabric adhesive
spray

Water-soluble
vanishing fabric in
various thicknesses

Embroidery hoop

Sewing threads

Water-soluble
vanishing thread

Pins

Thimble

Tape measure

Machine
needles

Water-soluble pen

Tailor's chalk pencil

Embroidery and
sewing needles

Water-soluble pencil

Dressmaker's carbon paper

basic

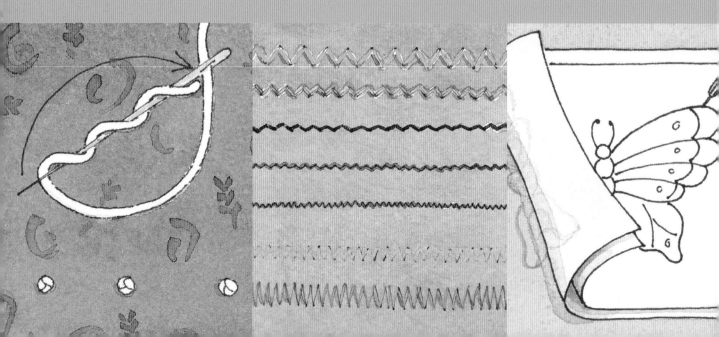

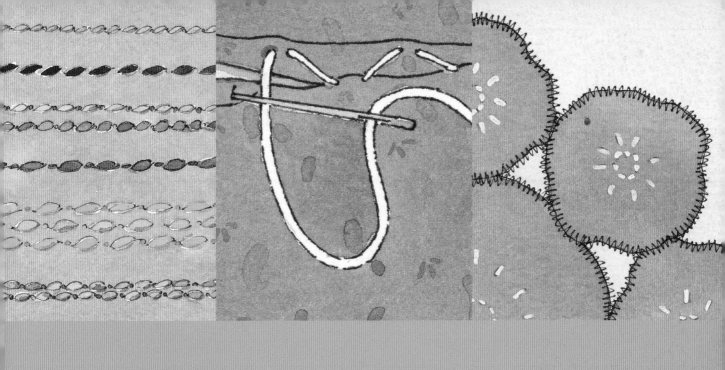

skills

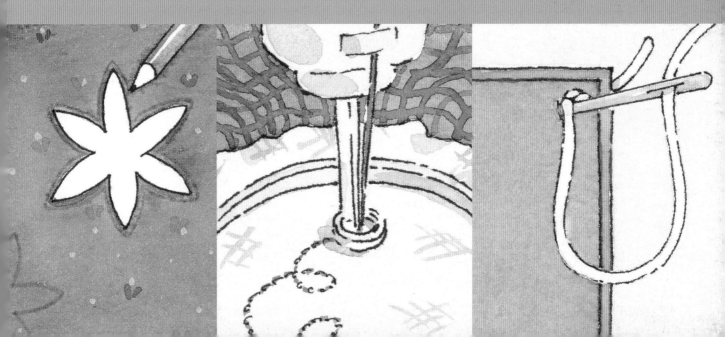

preparation

To make the embroidery process easier and more enjoyable, ensure that all the right equipment is at hand before starting. Assemble everything necessary and place it on a shelf or in a large box. If you are naturally impatient, like me, you may be tempted to ignore this advice. However, there is nothing more annoying than starting on a project and discovering, after the stores have closed, that an essential piece of equipment is missing.

It is also a good idea to prepare a work space in advance. You will need a clean, clear surface to work on and a steam iron and ironing board set up nearby. A sewing machine is a must, but nothing fancy is required. A simple machine that can zigzag is all you will need to make all the projects in this book. Make sure that you are familiar with the machine, and understand how it works. If you haven't used it for a while, then take a test run on some fabrics scraps. Check that there are extra machine needles at hand, in case of breakage.

cutting fabric

Most of the fabric pieces for the projects in this book are simple squares, rectangles, and strips. For straight pieces like this, you can use either sharp dressmaker's shears or the rotary cutting equipment used for patchworks.

Always cut pieces lined up with the straight grain of the fabric parallel to the selvages (the edges of the fabric), unless you are cutting bias strips for edgings, which are cut at a 45-degree angle to the selvage.

making paper patterns

If a project requires shaped pieces of fabric, such as the pieces for the chair-seat pad on page 32 or the hot water bottle cover on page 100, it is advisable to make a paper pattern as a guide to cutting. Paper patterns can be made out of special sewing pattern paper (covered with inch-based graph lines), brown paper, wallpaper, or any other large paper you have at hand.

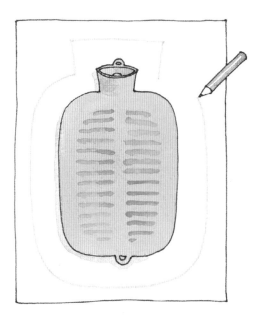

To make a paper pattern, draw the shape to the dimensions given in the instructions, adding the seam allowances. For some items, such as a hot water bottle cover (see above), use the object you are covering as your template, making sure you add the suggested seam allowance. Draw the straight lines using a ruler and the curves using a plate, glass, or bowl to achieve accurate outlines.

Paper patterns are handy because they can be used again and again. It is even worthwhile making them for simple fabric pieces, such as those for cushions. That way you won't have to work out the dimensions when you want to repeat the project. Once you have a whole collection of handmade patterns, you'll be able to whip up gifts in no time at all.

transferring a design

Some of the designs in this book are made with the aid of the templates that are provided on pages 106 and 107. You can either trace these onto tracing paper or photocopy them, then cut them out. (Use a photocopier to enlarge templates that are not provided at actual size.) Then trace around the template shape onto stiff, thin cardboard (card stock will do), and cut it out.

Transfer the template shape onto the fabric by carefully tracing around it using a water-soluble pen or pencil, or a tailor's chalk pencil (see below).

If the embroidery design is more complex (like the design for the butterfly picture on pages 40–43), transferring it onto the fabric is a little trickier. If the fabric is transparent, simply put your design underneath the fabric and trace the outlines with a water-soluble pen or a tailor's chalk pencil. If the fabric is opaque, transfer the design using dressmaker's carbon paper, which comes in a range of colors. Use it in the same way you would normal carbon paper; if the lines are faint, redraw them with a tailor's chalk pencil.

preparing an embroidery hoop

An embroidery hoop is an indispensable item for a sewing box. It is used for both hand and machine embroidery. There are many types of frames on the market now, and I am sure that with some investigation you will find the type that suits you best. For the projects in this book, I used a wooden hoop. Make sure your hoop is large enough to allow you to stitch freely within it. I generally use a hoop measuring 8–10in (20–25cm) in diameter.

Spending a little time binding the two wooden rings of the embroidery hoop is worth the effort. A bound hoop is a lot kinder to your work, is more secure, and will not leave marks on the fabric. Using bias binding or cut strips of calico, tightly bind the hoop (see below). Secure the ends with a few hand stitches.

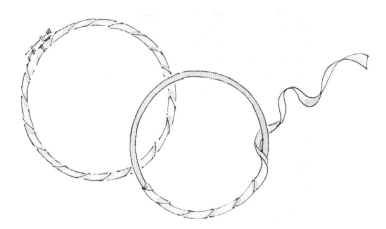

using an embroidery hoop

For successful embroidery, the fabric must be stretched very tightly on the embroidery hoop, so its surface is like a drum. This tight stretch is particularly important for machine embroidery. If the fabric is slack, the machine will miss stitches and the fabric might pucker.

To mount fabric in a hoop, first adjust the tension screw on the outer ring. Then place the outer ring on a flat surface and the fabric on top of it. Push the inner ring down into the outer one with the fabric in between. Pull the fabric upward and inward to tighten.

When stretching hand embroidery, place the fabric right side face down on the outer ring (see below); and for machine embroidery, right side face up (see below), so that the fabric will rest flat against the machine.

For hand embroidery

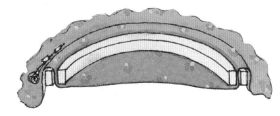

For machine embroidery

using water-soluble fabric

Water-soluble fabric is a fabric that washes away when soaked and rinsed in water. It can be covered with machine stitches and rinsed away to leave a lace fabric (see the bowls on pages 90–95). You can also draw the design on it, place it on your fabric, stitch over the design outline (see below), and rinse it away. This is particularly useful on textured fabrics like velvet, which are difficult to embroider onto directly. I have used water-soluble fabric for the flowers on pages 56–61, to hold the tiny shapes in place for embroidery.

There are many different types of water-soluble vanishing fabric available in craft and sewing stores. Its development has opened up a world of possibilities to the embroiderer. You can even buy water-soluble thread now for basting.

For the embroidered flowers and the machine-lace bowls, I have used a very thick water-soluble fabric. This type is a transparent film that takes a long time to wash out, which allows you to dry the embroidery while it is still sticky with the remaining film. The embroidery fabric will then be stiff when dry—perfect for firm fabric flowers and lace bowls.

If you are making a project for which you would like the finished work to drape, use a thinner water-soluble fabric that will wash out far more quickly and completely.

using fabric adhesive spray

If you want to avoid the stiffness of fusible bonding web adhesive (see next page) and want to hold fabrics together only temporarily, use fabric adhesive spray. This is widely used by quilters, who use it to secure the layers of the quilt together quickly and easily before quilting.

Temporary fabric adhesive spray is a really useful tool that eliminates the need for basting, and it is easy to wash out. You can use it to secure appliqué in position before it is stitched in place. It is also ideal for temporarily fixing layers of fabric together for the technique used for the hot water bottle cover on pages 100–103.

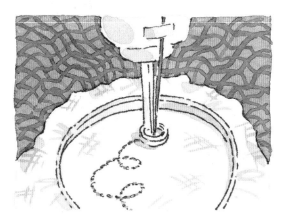

using fusible bonding web

Fusible bonding web is a web of adhesive with a paper backing. It is used to fuse two pieces of fabric together permanently and is transferred to fabric with the heat of an iron. This type of adhesive is fantastic for appliqué, since it basically makes fabric shapes into iron-on stickers. It also makes the fabric appliqué pieces firm and prevents the edges from fraying.

Although bonding web makes fabric rather stiff, you can turn this into an advantage, as I have done with the several projects. For example, the doilies on pages 86–89 and the butterfly picture on pages 40–43 benefit from the stiffness the adhesive gives them.

USING FUSIBLE BONDING WEB

1 Trace the design onto the paper side of the bonding web adhesive and cut out the shape. (You can cut the shape when it is fused in place, but this wastes fusible web.)

2 Place the adhesive-coated side face down on the wrong side of the appliqué fabric and press, carefully following the manufacturer's instructions.

3 Cut out the shape and peel off the paper backing.

4 Place the appliqué shape adhesive-side down on the ground fabric. Cover with a damp cloth and press firmly, again following the manufacturer's instructions.

1

2

3

4

basic hand stitching

There are times when completing a project that a little hand stitching is required. To an impatient embroiderer, this might sound too time consuming, but hand stitching is only suggested when it is the best way to obtain a nice-looking finish.

Use a good-quality thread for permanent hand stitching; you can use any thread for temporary basting. Find a color of thread that matches your fabric as closely as possible or is slightly darker. When choosing a thread color, always unwind a single thread and lay it on the fabric to check the match.

If you are right handed, stitch from right to left. It is best to use a length of thread about 18in (45cm) long. Before starting hand stitching, secure the thread with a few tiny stitches worked in the same place (see below), and do the same at the end of the stitching.

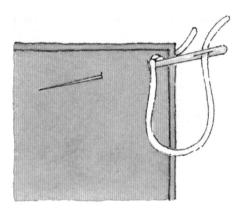

hand stitches

Only the most basic hand stitches are used for the designs in this book, and they are all shown here—running stitch, backstitch, slip stitch, overcast stitch, and ladder stitch. If you have never hand stitched, practice these stitches on pieces of scrap fabric before attempting to use them on the real thing. They are very easy to learn and will be useful for future embroidery and sewing projects. Just a little practice is enough to give you the skill required.

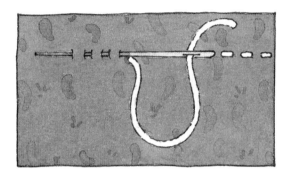

RUNNING STITCH

Running stitch is the simplest of all basic hand stitches. It can be used for seams or to gather fabric, for example for skirt tops or ruffles. Long running stitches are used for temporary basting, as the long stitches are easy to pull out once the machine stitching is complete.

To work running stitch, move the needle in and out of the fabric until there are several stitches on the needle (see above), then pull the needle through.

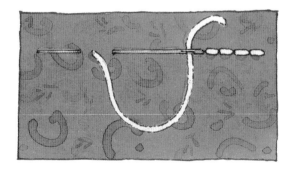

BACKSTITCH

Backstitch is used for making strong seams, as it holds the layers of fabric firmly together so that they will not pull apart.

To start the stitch, make one small stitch from right to left. Bring the needle up a short distance to the left of the first stitch. Insert the needle in same place as the end of the previous stitch and bring it forward a stitch length farther to create an unbroken line of stitches (see above).

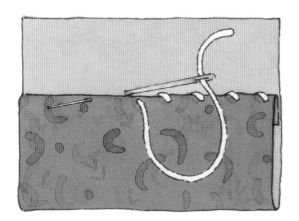

SLIP STITCH

To hem edges of fabric, you need to make stitches that are tiny enough to be invisible on the right side of the fabric. There are many forms of hemming stitches, but the one shown here (see above), called slip stitch, is the easiest.

To make a hem, first fold under ¼in (6mm) to the wrong side along the raw edge of the fabric and press. Then make another fold along the desired hemline and press again. Pin the hem in place. With the wrong side of the item facing you, work slip stitches along the first fold as shown (see above), making only tiny stitches through the bottom layer of fabric.

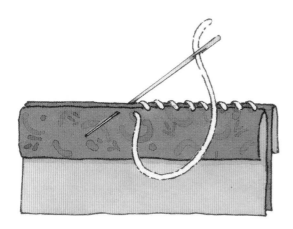

OVERCAST STITCH

Overcast stitch, also known as oversewing, is handy for joining two folds of fabric together (see above). With practice, it can be worked quite quickly. Start the stitch in the usual way, making a few tiny stitches in the same place to secure the

thread (knots can work free, so they are not recommended when you need a strong seam). Insert the needle through both folds near the edge for each stitch.

You can work overcast stitch on the right or wrong side of the fabric, but if you are using it on the right side of the fabric, be sure to take care to form more regular, neat stitches as they will be visible.

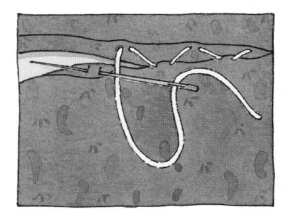

LADDER STITCH

Ladder stitch is an invisible method of closing an opening in a seam. For example, it can be used to close an opening that has been left in a seam so that the item can be turned right-side out through the gap in the stitching.

To work ladder stitch, first fold a crease in each layer of fabric along the seam line so you can stitch from one fold to the other. Pick up a tiny piece of the fabric just inside one fold line, then pick up another just inside the other fold line (see above). As you pull the thread gently, the small stitches will close the opening invisibly.

hand embroidery

At certain times, even if you are impatient, you might want to hand embroider. To be honest, there is no shortcut to hand stitching, but practice definitely improves both skill and speed.

It is all too tempting to start and finish embroidery with a knot. In some cases, this method is quick and acceptable. However, a knot is not entirely secure and can be unsightly and add bulk to your work. To make a neater start to hand embroidery, there are other options that take a little more time but ensure a better finish. Of course, the method you choose will depend entirely on the type of embroidery and the item you are embroidering. Sometimes when embroidering an

edging, a few tiny stitches at the beginning and end of the stitching are best for securing the ends. On other occasions, it is better to leave tails of thread that can be darned into the back of the embroidery later.

When preparing thread for embroidery, cut lengths of about 18in (45cm). Longer lengths are difficult to handle. The hand-embroidered designs in this book all use cotton embroidery floss. This is slightly lustrous and comprises of six strands, which can be used together (as I have used them) or separated to produce thinner threads. The key to needle choice is to make sure your thread slips easily through both the eye of the needle and the fabric you are stitching.

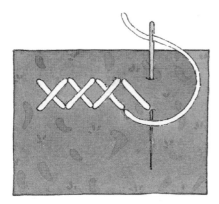

CROSS-STITCH

This stitch is formed by a series of equal-length stitches that cross each other diagonally. It is important that all the top stitches slant in the same direction (see above).

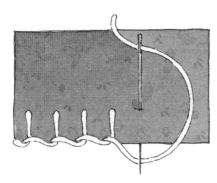

BLANKET STITCH

This is an edging stitch (see above). When the stitches are worked close together it is called buttonhole stitch.

FEATHER STITCH

For this decorative stitch, make a slanting stitch (see above), then loop the thread under the needle and pull it through. Make the next stitch on the other side in the same way.

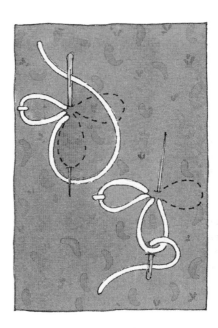

LAZY DAISY STITCH

This is an elaborate version of traditional chain stitch, a commonly used looped stitch. In lazy daisy stitch, each chain loop is secured at the end with an extra stitch (see above). It is ideal for depicting petals.

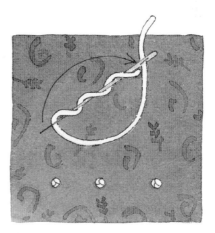

FRENCH KNOTS

These are great raised stitches that look like little beads. Wind the needle around the thread a few times before passing it back through the fabric next to the point where it first emerged. It takes a little practice, but is quick once you master it.

sewing machine basics

Sewing machines vary so much that it is important to refer to the machine manual for specific instructions on how to use your machine. Because of these variations, only the most basic parts and functions of the machine are given here.

To familiarize yourself with your machine, practice winding the bobbin, threading the top of the machine, and inserting the bobbin. (When inserting the bobbin, make sure the thread is winding around it in the direction shown in the machine manual.) Then try working a simple straight stitch on scrap fabric with any color sewing thread. First, insert the fabric under the needle, then lower the large lever at the side or back of the needle to lower the presser foot so that the fabric is gripped between the teeth (the feed dogs) under the throat plate and the presser foot. The needle will then bring the top thread down through the fabric and the throat plate underneath so that the top thread is linked with the bobbin thread. Change the tension dial and the stitch-length dial to see how this alters the look of the stitch.

You should always do a practice sample when using new fabric and new threads in order to check the stitch tension. Incorrect thread tension is one of the main reasons for frustration when machine stitching. Years ago, when I first started using the sewing machine, I would virtually be in tears with broken threads and missed stitches everywhere, swearing that I would hand stitch everything in the future.

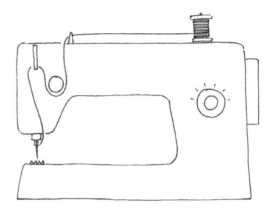

Follow the machine manual to thread the machine

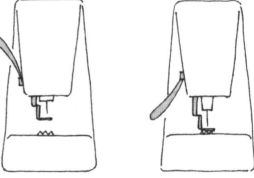

Presser foot lifted   **Presser foot lowered**

Upper thread too loose or bobbin thread too tight

Bobbin thread too loose or upper thread too tight

Correct tension—both threads in correct position

correct and incorrect tension

To ensure that the machine is stitching to the correct tension, before you begin a project, thread the machine with the thread you will be using. Then stitch a few sample lines on a scrap of the fabric you will be using. If the upper thread is too loose or the bobbin thread too tight, the top thread will be pulled too far through to the back of the fabric. If the bobbin thread is too loose or the upper tension too tight, the reverse will occur. Aim for equal tension on both upper and lower threads.

machine stitched seams

When machine stitching a seam, remember to check that the sewing tension is correct for the fabric you are using before starting a project (see previous page). Test this on a scrap of fabric as explained. I often forget to do this and then have to unpick stitching, which is really tedious. On the subject of avoiding undoing seams, always double-check that you are stitching the right pieces together with the correct sides of the fabric facing each other; it is so easy to make mistakes. For seams, use a standard ½in (1.5cm) seam allowance.

For items that are going to be washed regularly, it is advisable to finish the raw edges. I often use the old-fashioned method of pinking raw edges with a pair of pinking shears, but a machine-zigzagged edge is more robust. Remember to press seams open as you go.

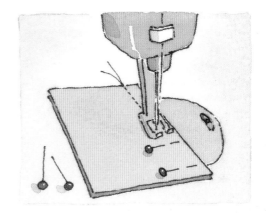

machine stitching

1 Before machine stitching, pin the fabric pieces to each other with the right sides together and the raw edges aligned. (If there are more than two layers of fabric or the fabric pieces need more stability, baste them together with long running stitches and remove the pins before stitching. It is easier if you are a beginner to baste all seams first rather than to try removing pins before the machine needle reaches them.) With the machine set at 10–12 stitches to 1in (2.5cm), machine stitch with the pins at right angles to the seam line, removing the pins before the needle reaches them (see top right).

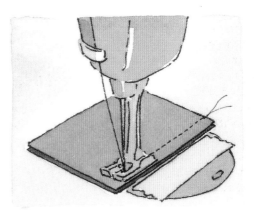

2 To make an even seam line, keep the edge of the fabric aligned with one of the seam guides on the machine, or place masking tape on the throat plate at the correct distance from the needle and keep the fabric edge aligned with it (see middle right).

3 When stitching around a corner, keep the needle down at the corner point, lift the presser foot, pivot the fabric (see bottom right), then lower the presser foot and continue.

machine embroidery

Machine embroidery offers all sorts of exciting possibilities for design, but for the purposes of this book, I have kept the range limited and the stitches very simple so that the techniques are easy to pick up. You can choose between two different methods of machine embroidery: one method employs ordinary machine straight and zigzag stitches and the other uses free-motion stitches (see pages 26 and 27) in which you, rather than the machine, control the movement of the stitches over the fabric.

For a long time, I owned only a straight-stitch machine. The constraint of having only one stitch to work with gave me the chance to fully explore its design uses. In the last few years, however, I have branched out and purchased a machine with a zigzag stitch. This is not only a useful decorative stitch but is also fantastic for finishing raw edges on seams.

An embroiderer friend says she particularly likes using wide, closely worked zigzag stitch in her work—also known as machine satin stitch—because it allows her to produce striking bold lines of color. Machine stitching has endless variations, and once you have mastered the basics, you can play with textured, smooth, and glittery threads to create all sorts of interesting stitches and combinations.

straight stitching

Do not be tempted to ignore the straight machine stitching used for sewing seams as a form of decorative embroidery. To vary the look, you can alter the stitch length or use a thicker thread, such as dressmaker's buttonhole thread, threaded through the top of the machine.

It is important to recognize that you can use embroidery threads in your sewing machine as well as standard cotton sewing threads and machine threads. Although these are too thick to pass through the machine needle, they can be used as the bobbin thread.

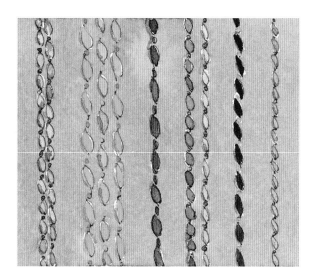

Above: Straight stitches in different lengths worked with threads of various thicknesses. When using thread that is too thick for the top of the machine, use on the bobbin instead and machine stitch with the right side of the fabric facing down.

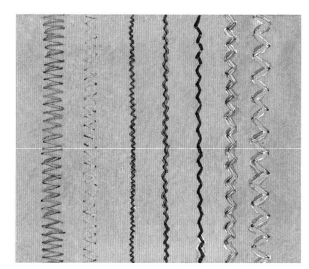

Above: Zigzag stitches worked in different widths and lengths, using thin and thick threads. As for straight stitches, wind threads around the bobbin if they are too thick for the needle.

WORKING WITH THICK EMBROIDERY THREADS

To use embroidery threads, such as pearl cotton or stranded embroidery floss, hand wind the thread onto the bobbin. Then loosen the bobbin tension until the thread glides through comfortably. Thread the top of the machine with an ordinary matching sewing thread.

Since the "couched" threads (the bobbin threads) will form on the bottom of the fabric, insert the fabric under the sewing machine needle with the right side of the fabric facing the throat plate and the wrong side of the fabric face up. Work some test stitching and adjust the tension to perfect it.

zigzag stitching

The zigzag stitch on the sewing machine can be worked with the stitches wide apart, for a decorative zigzag effect or to finish raw edges, or close together to create a satin-stitch-like effect. The broad line of color created with machine satin stitch is perfect for edging appliqué or for cutwork edges like those on the doilies on pages 86–89.

WORKING MACHINE SATIN STITCH

For machine satin stitch (see below), set the stitch width to the widest it will go and the stitch length to almost zero, but not quite or the machine will not move the fabric along at all. It is advisable to back fine fabrics with a stabilizer, as this stitch can sometimes pucker the fabric. I have recently

discovered water-soluble vanishing fabric which works well as a stabilizer and has the added advantage of disappearing when rinsed in water (see page 16). This second feature is particularly useful for cutwork edgings.

TURNING CORNERS WITH ZIGZAG STITCH

The thing to practice when using machine satin stitch is turning a corner. There are many ideas on how best to do this. My theory is to approach the corner slowly and perform the last few stitches manually if necessary, then carefully lift both the needle and presser foot, turn the fabric, and reposition

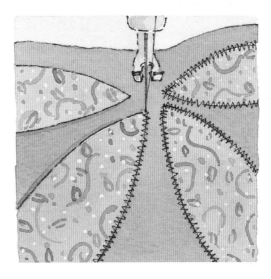

the needle and presser foot (see above). Just be very careful to avoid pulling either the top or bottom threads, since this can cause an unsightly loop on the stitch surface or possibly even jam the machine.

If my method of turning does not work for you, turn the fabric with the needle still in the fabric, then lift it, adjust its position, lower the presser foot, and continue. With a little practice you will master it.

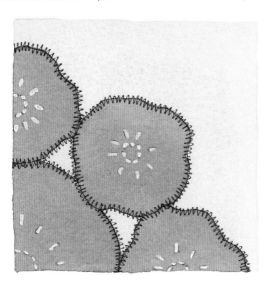

free-motion machine embroidery

Free-motion embroidery is a little more difficult to learn than ordinary machine stitching, but give it a try if you haven't already. It gives you the scope to stitch in any direction, rather like drawing with a needle. In free-motion machine embroidery, the teeth that grip and move the fabric in normal machine stitching are disengaged so that you can move the fabric yourself to control the path of the stitches.

When I started to experiment with free-motion embroidery, I spent some time playing with different thicknesses of thread without any lessons at all. Basically, there was a lot of trial and error and some amazing happy accidents. These accidents that I thought were my very own inventions I later found in embroidery books!

PREPARING FOR FREE-MOTION EMBROIDERY

When working free-motion machine embroidery, you should usually stretch the fabric on a hoop to keep it taut (see pages 15 and 16). If the fabric is thick, quilted, or backed, however, it will be firm enough to stitch without an embroidery frame.

Start preparing your machine for free-motion embroidery by inserting a medium-size (80/12) needle. Very thin needles are not strong enough to stand up to machine embroidery.

Next, remove the regular presser foot from the machine and replace it with a darning foot. The look of the darning foot varies, but it is essentially a ring of metal. The darning foot is not pressed onto the fabric like an ordinary presser foot, so it is possible to free-motion embroider without any foot at all. If you are new to machine embroidery, though, I advise you to use one, as it will help to protect your fingers.

Remember to disengage the feed dogs before beginning. (Consult the sewing machine manual, as the method of disengaging the feed dogs varies from machine to machine.) Before you begin stitching a project, practice free-motion stitching on a piece of spare fabric.

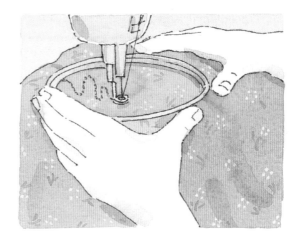

PRACTICING

1 Insert the fabric under the needle and darning foot, and place it flat against the throat plate. Lower the presser foot lever. (Always lower the presser foot lever even though the darning foot does not grip the fabric, as this engages the top thread's tension.) Hold the top thread, lower the needle manually through the fabric, and draw the bobbin thread to the top. Pull the end of the bobbin thread up through the fabric. Hold both threads and work a few stitches, then snip off the thread ends. First, try working a curvy line (see top right). The length of the stitches is determined by a combination of how quickly you move the fabric and the machine speed. If you don't keep the fabric moving, the machine will stitch over and over in one place and the needle will jam.

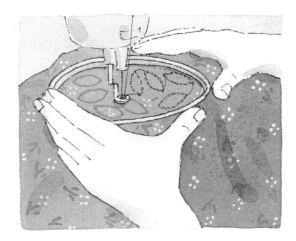

2 Next, try working petal shapes (see middle right). To move from one part of the work to another, first lift up the needle as high as it will go and then lift up the presser foot lever to take the strain off the needle. Move the hoop across to the desired position and lower the needle manually into the fabric. Then lower the presser foot lever and continue sewing. If you move the work a big distance, dip the needle into the fabric once, then reposition it—the floating threads are cut off later. In order to prevent stiches from unraveling once the threads are cut, make sure that the first and last stitches are small.

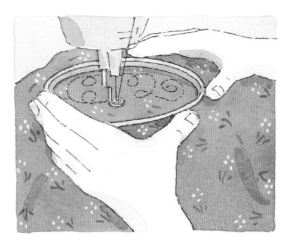

3 Lastly, try creating a whole surface of overlapping stitches (see bottom right) on water-soluble vanishing fabric (as for the bowl on page 90). Make sure the stitches overlap so that when you rinse out the fabric, the stitches are linked.

finishing touches

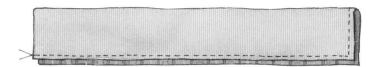

fabric tubes

If you have never learned how to make a tube of fabric, now is the time. It is a basic sewing method that you can use to make such things as ties (see the quilted chair-seat pad on pages 32–35) and straps (see the cross-stitch handbag on pages 48–51). The width and length of the tube varies according to its use.

1 To start, cut the fabric to twice the desired finished width of the tube, plus seam allowances, and to the desired length, plus seam allowances (see top left). (The project instructions for fabric tubes in this book provide the precise strip measurements required.)

2 Fold the fabric strip in half lengthwise with right sides together and press. Pin the layers together and machine stitch around the edge (see middle left), leaving one end open.

3 Turn the tube right-side out (see bottom left). To do this, either attach a safety pin to one end and use it to draw the fabric through, or poke the end through with the blunt end of a knitting needle. Press the tube flat, aligning the seam with one edge. Turn under the raw edge at the end, press, and stitch.

BAG HANDLES

If you are adding handles to a simple bag, make the tubes of fabric to the appropriate width and length as shown above. Remember that they will need to be wide enough and strong enough to support heavy weight, and therefore need to be stitched firmly to the bag fabric (ideally padded to provide support for the stitching).

Sew the handles securely in place by first stitching a square and then stitching across the square diagonally in both directions (see left). Then continue following the instructions for the relevant project.

binding with mitered corners

The following instructions are for a self-bound edging with mitered corners—miters are seams stitched in corners at a 45-degree angle. For this edging, the backing fabric is folded over onto the right side of the front fabric to bind the edge, but you can adapt the principle by turning the top fabric to the wrong side over the backing if you prefer. A handy finishing technique, self-bound edging is ideal for throws, placemats, and tablecloths.

When cutting the backing fabric, make sure that it is wider than the front fabric. Allow for the finished width of the binding, plus extra for the turn-under. It is easiest to allow for more than you need and then trim the backing to the correct width right before starting the binding.

Ensure that the width of the binding is in keeping with the scale of the project. For example, for a large tablecloth, allow at least a 1in (2.5cm) binding and add ¼in (6mm) extra for turning under along the raw edges.

STITCHING A MITERED BINDING

1 Trim the lining to the required width of the finished binding plus a turn-under allowance. Clip off the corner of the trimmed border fabric so that it will not poke out past the binding when folded over.

2 Fold each corner point over to the right side of the patchwork top.

3 Fold under ¼in (6mm) along the raw edges and pin in place along one side.

4 Continue pinning around the edge, carefully matching the folded edges at the corners.

5 Slip stitch the binding in place along the fold line.

6 Slip stitch the mitered corners where the angled edges meet.

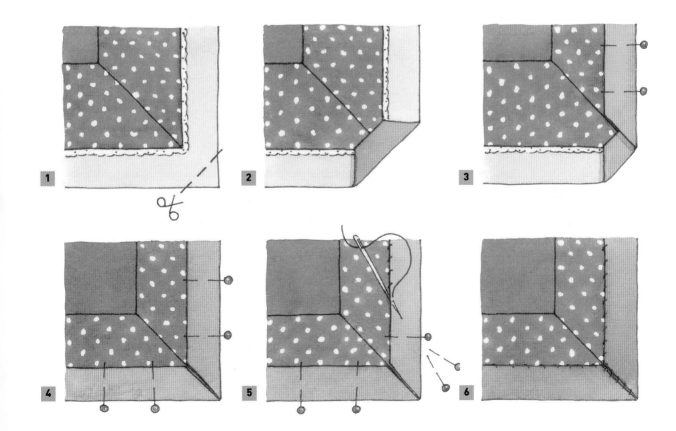

project

gallery

quilted chair-
seat pad

Making this seat pad is a really good introduction to free-motion machine embroidery. The quilting pattern I have used is called "vermicelli " or "stipple" quilting. This simple technique involves allowing the machine needle to wander about in one continuous line to form random meandering curved lines. Experiment on scraps of fabric before you start; the key is to relax and not make any sudden or jerky movements. It is best to start and finish the quilting stitches at the edge of the fabric so that there are no line breaks in the middle of the seat pad.

Of course, every chair is different, so start by making a template for a pad that will fit your chair. Where you position the ties will also depend on the design of the chair back.

If you don't feel confidant to free-motion machine quilt your cushion, why not quilt straight lines or mix straight horizontal and vertical lines for checks? Buy a fabric that matches your color scheme and you will soon be on your way to making a whole set of seat pads at a fraction of the price you would pay for similar ones in the stores.

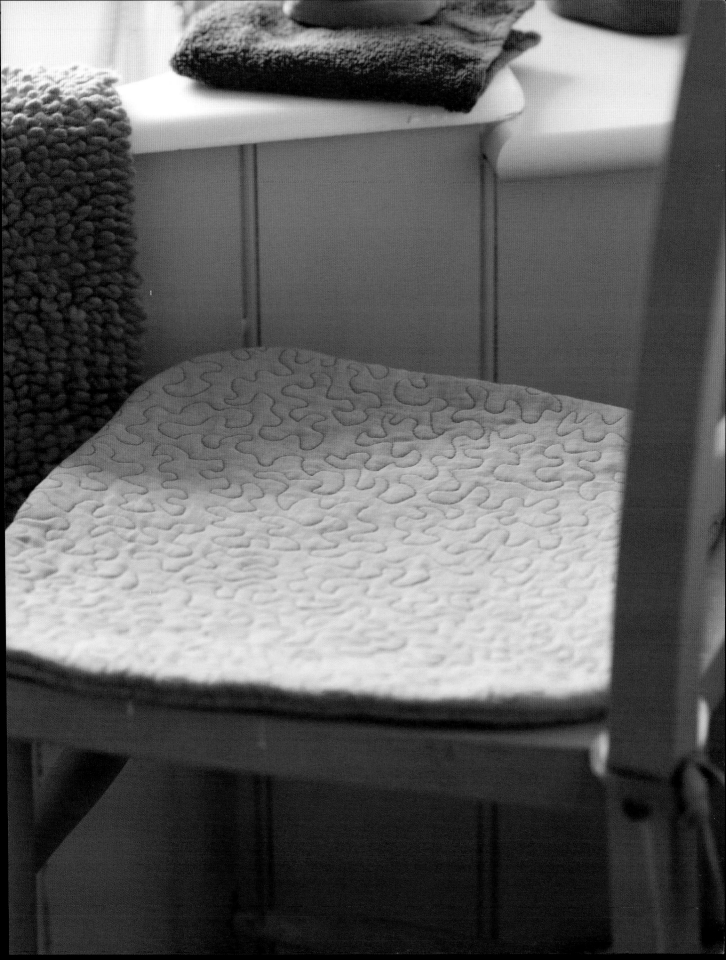

how to make the chair-seat pad

It is worth taking the time to make a template and paper pattern for your chair-seat pad so that it will fit the chair properly. A good template is especially important if you are making pads for a set of chairs.

Measure and draw the chair-seat shape very carefully when following step 1. After cutting out the template shape (before making the final pattern with the seam allowance), lay it on the chair to ensure that it's the right size. If it isn't quite right, redo it until it is perfect. This doesn't take as long as it might sound and will give much better results.

materials

For each finished chair-seat pad for a standard-size chair, you will need:
³/₄yd (70cm) each of two 44in (112cm) wide cotton fabrics as follows—
A = solid-color (ROWAN *Shot Cotton* SC41)
B = ecru calico or muslin for the backing
Lightweight batting, 22in by 44in (56cm by 112cm) square
Fabric adhesive spray for basting (optional)
Matching or contrasting machine thread for quilting
Matching thread for sewing cover together

quilting the seat pad

1 To make a paper pattern for the pad, first make an exact template of the chair seat. Measure the seat and draw its outline on a large piece of paper (if you prefer a pad slightly smaller than the seat, draw the outline accordingly). To round off the two front corners of the template, draw a curve at one corner, tracing around the edge of a plate, bowl, or glass (find an object that matches the curve of your chair seat or that flatters the chair-seat shape). For a perfectly symmetrical template, fold the drawing of the template in half and cut it out, carefully following the marked curved line at the front corner. Mark the position for the two ties on the template. Trace this seat template onto another piece of paper to make a pattern piece. Add an extra ³/₄in (2cm) all around the shape for a generous seam allowance, and cut out the pattern piece.

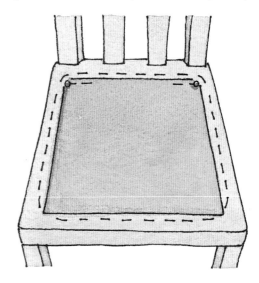

2 Using the paper pattern piece, cut out two pieces from fabric A (the solid-colored fabric), two from the batting, and two from fabric B (the calico backing). Lay the pieces on top of each other in two identical stacks—one for the front of the pad and one for the back. Place the calico backing on the bottom of each stack, the batting in the middle, and the solid-colored fabric on top with the right side facing up. Baste or spray glue the layers of each stack together.

3 Put the darning presser foot on your sewing machine and disengage the feed dogs so the machine is ready for free-motion embroidery. Using a matching or contrasting thread and a straight machine stitch, free-motion stitch a vermicelli pattern on the back and front pieces. Let your machine wander in one continuous line to cover the entire piece. Alternatively, you can work in a few separate continuous lines, but always start and stop the stitching near the edge (see below).

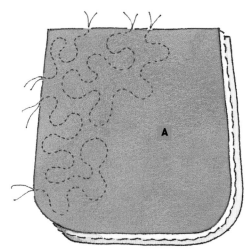

2 Using the template that is the same size as the chair seat and a water-soluble pen or tailor's chalk pencil, trace the seat shape on the wrong side (the calico side) of one of the quilted pieces and mark the position for the ties. Pin and baste the front to the back, with the right sides together and the ties sandwiched between them. Machine stitch the pieces together along the marked line, leaving an opening between the ties (see below). Remove the basting.

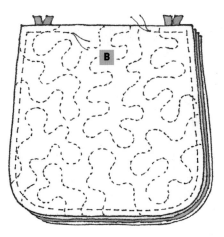

3 Trim the seam allowances to ¼in (6mm) and turn the cover right-side out. Ladder stitch the opening closed (see below).

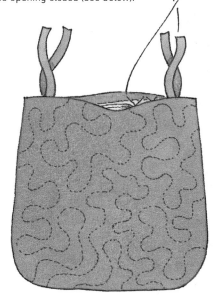

finishing the seat pad

1 Make the four ties for the seat pad. For each pair of ties, cut a strip 24in by 2in (60cm by 4cm) from fabric A. Fold under and press ½in (1cm) along each long edge of the strip. Then fold under ½in (1cm) at each end and press. Lastly, fold the strip in half lengthwise, pin, and baste. Using a matching thread, machine topstitch all around three sides of the tie, stitching close to the edge. Cut each tie in half.

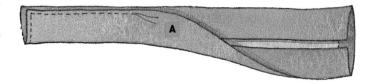

chair-back cover

I used a striped fabric as a guide for the straight embroidery lines on this chair-back cover. I often place a patterned fabric—floral, stripes, or checks—on the back of the fabric I am embroidering, to use as a guide for machine embroidery. As long as you work the machine embroidery with the wrong side of the fabric facing you and don't mind the extra thickness another layer of fabric will give to your finished piece, it works like a charm. The bobbin thread on the right side of the fabric forms the finished embroidery.

When you use a thick thread for machine embroidery, as on this cover, always hand wind your bobbin (see page 25). You do have to rewind the bobbin frequently, but the embroidery texture makes it worthwhile—the results look like a lot like hand couching.

I started this project thinking I would just create a pinstripe design and then got thoroughly carried away experimenting with color and design. The final piece has an air of vintage deckchair fabric to it.

how to make the chair-back cover

A striped fabric is used as a guide for the embroidered straight lines on this cover. This striped fabric is hidden inside the cover once the backing is stitched on.

Work the embroidered stripes in any sequence or pattern you like. Stitch them exactly on the line between two fabric stripes or in the exact middle of a fabric stripe. If you want to try the stripe sequence I used, as shown on page 37, here it is. Starting with the embroidered stripe at the center of the cover, the sequence from the center to the outer edge on one side is as follows:
Yellow (center stripe), 1/4in (6mm) gap, orange, 1/4in (6mm) gap, light blue, 1/4in (6mm) gap, dark blue, 1/2in (12mm) gap, green, 1 1/4in (3cm) gap, yellow, 1 1/4in (3cm) gap, green, 1/2in (12mm) gap, dark blue, 1/4in (6mm) gap, light blue, 1/4in (6mm) gap, orange, 1/4in (6mm) gap; repeat from * to * once more. For the other side, echo this sequence for a mirror image of stripes, starting with orange next to the central yellow stripe.

materials

For a finished chair-back cover measuring approximately 21in by 15in (53cm by 38cm), you will need:
1/2yd (45cm) of each of three 44in (112cm) wide cotton fabrics as follows—
    A = solid color (ROWAN *Shot Cotton* SC01) for the front of the cover
    B = woven stripe with 1/2in (12mm) stripes (ROWAN *Single Ikat Feathers* in any shade) for the stitching guide
    C = second solid color (ROWAN *Shot Cotton* SC21) for the backing
Fabric spray adhesive for basting
Three skeins each of five colors of six-stranded cotton embroidery floss (ANCHOR green No. 255, dark blue No. 169, light blue No. 1032, orange No. 925, and yellow No. 303)
Machine thread in five colors to match the five embroidery floss colors
Machine thread that matches the backing fabric

stitching the cover

1 Cut a rectangle 21in by 15in (53cm by 38cm) from fabric A for the front of the cover (see below). Cut another rectangle the same size from fabric B (the stripe), cutting so that the stripes run lengthwise.

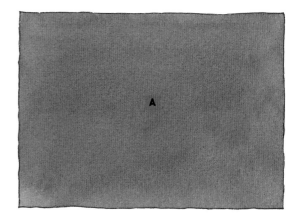

2 With a water-soluble vanishing pen, mark the positions of the embroidered stripes on the right side of fabric B, using the fabric stripes as a guide (see below). Mark the color next to each stripe position—G for green, DB for dark blue, and so on. (See the introduction on the left for the stripe sequence.)

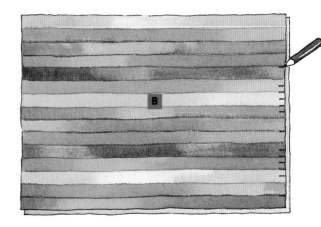

3 With wrong sides together, spray baste fabric B to fabric A. Then thread the top of your sewing machine with the machine thread that matches the central embroidered stripe. Using all six strands of the embroidery floss together, hand wind the floss for the central stripe onto the sewing machine bobbin (the bobbin will sew two lines of stitching before it needs rethreading). With the stripe fabric face up, work one color at a time, from the center of the cover outward.

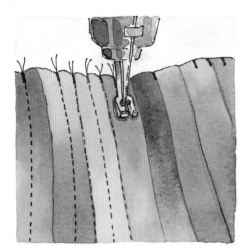

4 Press the finished embroidery. Then cut a rectangle 23¹/₂in by 17¹/₂in (59cm by 44cm) from fabric C for the backing—the backing should be 1¹/₄in (3cm) bigger all around than the front. Spray baste the embroidered front right-side up in the center of the wrong side of the backing (see below).

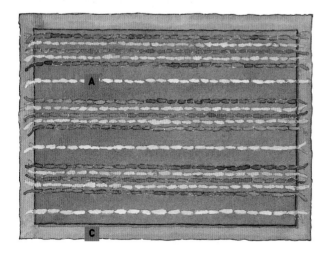

5 At each corner, fold the backing fabric to the front at an angle as shown (see below), and trim off the excess corner of backing fabric.

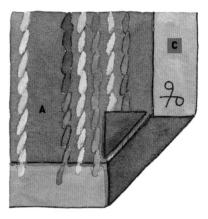

6 Fold under and press ⁵/₈in (1.5cm) all the way around the edge, one side at a time. Then turn under another ⁵/₈in (1.5cm) and pin and baste the border in place (see below). Topstitch close to the edge of the border and remove the basting (see page 29 for detailed instructions on making this type of border). Press the finished border.

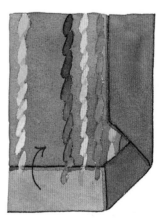

butterfly picture

Traditionally, elaborate motifs have been used in embroidery, but if you find the prospect of drawing and designing quite scary, you might shy away from them. There are, however, lots of ways of cheating. Embroidery books full of embroidery transfers are widely available; they are a wonderful source of imagery—from florals to fairies. I found the inspiration for this butterfly in a book of copyright-free embroidery transfers.

I included this machine- and hand-embroidered picture because it is a good exercise in transferring a design from paper to fabric. There are many methods of doing this, but after much research, I found that using dressmaker's carbon paper is an excellent way of transferring an image. And the outlines are easy to wash out afterward. Although this butterfly design is very simple, there is nothing stopping you from adorning yours with sequins and beads.

Mounting the finished machine-embroidered picture on a pre-stretched artist's canvas is the perfect quick-finishing technique for the impatient embroiderer.

how to make the butterfly picture

Don't worry about your stitches being too exact; the lines should look freely drawn rather than immaculate. Machine embroider all the butterfly outlines first, then hand embroider the pink dots with French knots.

materials

For a finished picture measuring 12in by 12in (30cm by 30cm), you will need:

1/2yd (45cm) each of two 44in (112cm) wide cotton fabrics as follows—

A = dark solid color (ROWAN *Shot Cotton* SC22), for butterfly

B = medium-toned solid color (ROWAN *Shot Cotton* SC18), for background

Dressmaker's carbon paper

10in (25cm) embroidery hoop

Thick white sewing thread for the butterfly

White cotton machine thread for the bobbin thread

Paper-backed fusible bonding web adhesive

One skein of six-stranded cotton embroidery floss (ANCHOR hot pink No. 62)

Pre-stretched artist's canvas, 12in by 12in (30cm by 30cm)

embroidering the picture

1 For the butterfly embroidery, cut a piece 16in by 16in (40cm by 40cm) from fabric A (the dark solid-colored fabric).

2 Enlarge the butterfly design (see page 107). Then lay the piece of fabric A on a flat surface, with the right side face up. Lay a piece of dressmaker's carbon paper in the center of the fabric, with the carbon side down. Finally, lay the butterfly design face up on top of the carbon paper. Pin all the layers together. Using a ballpoint pen, draw around the butterfly

outlines, pressing down firmly (see below). Remove the butterfly design and the carbon paper. If the outlines are a little faint, use a tailor's chalk pencil to embolden the lines.

3 Stretch the butterfly on an embroidery hoop with one wing in the center. Put the darning presser foot on your sewing machine and disengage the feed dogs so the machine is ready for free-motion embroidery. Thread thick white thread through the top of the machine and wind ordinary machine thread on the bobbin. Free-motion machine stitch the wing of the butterfly (see below). Once you have completed one wing, take the fabric out of the hoop, reposition it so that the other wing is in the center, and complete the embroidery.

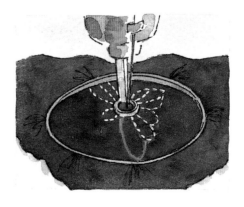

4 Press the finished machine embroidery. Then cut a square of fusible bonding web to the length and depth of the butterfly motif and fuse it to the wrong side of the embroidery, following the manufacturer's instructions. With the paper backing still in place on the bonding web, carefully cut out the butterfly motif (see below).

5 For the picture background, cut a piece of fabric B (the medium-toned solid-colored fabric) 16in by 16in (40cm by 40cm). Peel off the backing paper on the butterfly motif and place it adhesive-side down in the center of the background fabric. Iron on the motif, again carefully following the manufacturer's instructions (see below).

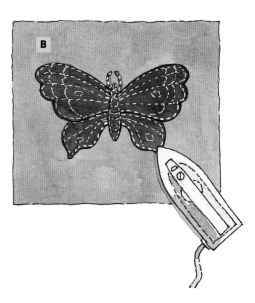

6 Lay the prepared embroidery wrong-side down on a flat surface. Place the stretched artist's canvas face down on top of it, carefully centering the canvas. Make sure the grain of the fabric is straight, then staple the fabric to back of the frame in the middle of one side. Pull the fabric tight and staple it in the middle of the opposite side. Repeat this process on the other two sides, making sure that the fabric is taut and the fabric grain is straight. Work outward toward the corners, stapling alternate sides as you go. At each corner, fold the loose fabric up to form a triangle, then back on itself and staple as shown (see below). Trim off the excess fabric.

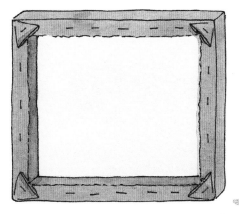

7 Work French knots on the wings using all six strands of the embroidery floss together (see below).

raw appliqué cushion

Raw-edge appliqué has become really fashionable for clothing, and there is no reason why this trend should not be transferred to home furnishings. This cushion design does bare some resemblance to patchwork, but on closer inspection you notice the lush appliqué texture created by the layers and the stitching. The shot cotton fabrics used look really good with frayed edges because the warp and weft are two different colors.

Make sure that you cut all the appliqué squares on the straight grain of the fabric so you have the option of neatly fraying the edges or leaving the process to occur naturally as I have done.

If you prefer an unfrayed finish, edge the squares with machine satin stitch instead (see pages 80 and 81), or bond the squares to the cushion with fusible bonding web, then topstitch them in place.

how to make the raw appliqué cushion

Use the Rowan fabric shades given below, or choose shades that better suit your decor. If you are selecting different solid colors, make sure they contrast enough to stand out against each other in the layered appliqué.

materials

For a finished cushion measuring approximately 20in by 20in (50cm by 50cm), you will need:
Five 44in (112cm) wide cotton fabrics as follows—
  A = 1yd (1m) of a medium-scale dot print (ROWAN *Roman Glass* G01BY) for the front and back
  B, C, D, and E = small amount each of four different solid colors (ROWAN *Shot Cotton* SC09 pomegranate, SC12 chartreuse, SC01 ginger, and SC17 sage)
Dark brown machine thread
Nine dark brown buttons, ⅝in (1.5cm) in diameter
Pillow form, 20in (50cm) square

working the machine appliqué

1 For the front of the cushion, cut a square 21in by 21in (53cm by 53cm) from fabric A (see below).

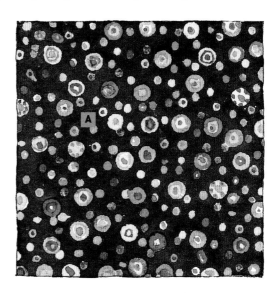

2 Using a rotary cutter, cut nine patches in each of four different sizes (see below). Use solid colored fabrics B, C, D, and E randomly; or to exactly match the cushion on page 44, follow the diagram on page 106 and cut patches as follows: For the 5½in (13.5cm) squares, cut three from fabric B, two from C, one from D, and three from E. For the 4½in (11.5cm) squares, cut two from fabric B, two from C, four from D, and one from E. For the 3½in (9cm) squares, cut two from fabric B, two from C, three from D, and two from E. For the 2½in (6cm) squares, cut two from fabric B, three from C, one from D, and three from E.

3 Arrange the nine largest squares in the center of the right side of the cushion front, leaving ¾in (2cm) gaps between them. Then position one of each of the next three sizes of squares on top of each large square, centering them on the square below. Pin, baste, then machine topstitch the squares in place, using a dark brown machine thread.

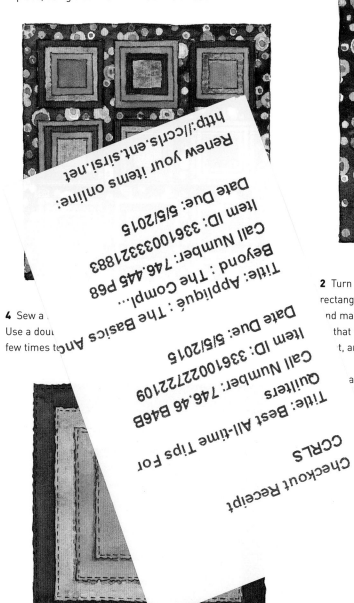

4 Sew a ...
Use a dou...
few times t...

sewing on the cushion back

1 For the cushion-cover back, cut out two rectangles each 21in by 13½in (53cm by 34cm) from fabric A (see below).

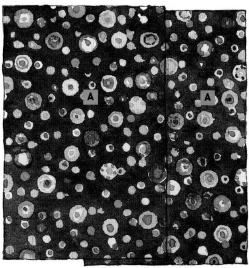

2 Turn under ½in (1.5cm) along one long edge of each rectangle to form a hem and press. Pin each hem in position ...nd machine stitch. Overlap the two back pieces by 5in (12cm) ...that they form a single piece the same size as the cushion ...t, and pin them together.

...and baste the cushion back pieces to the cushion front, ...ht sides together. Machine stitch, leaving a ½in ...eam allowance. Remove the basting.

...e crisp corners, clip off a triangle of the seam ...each of the four corners before turning the cover ...To do this, cut diagonally across the corner ...n) from the seam. Turn the cushion cover ...d insert the pillow form.

cross-stitch handbag

This handbag has a sort of faux smocked effect to it that is created with the help of a secret ingredient—curtain tape. If you have seen this tape before, you will know that using it is a really simple way of gathering fabric into perfectly uniform pleats.

The cross-stitch embroidery acts both as a decorative feature and as a way of holding the pleats in position. The gathers make the bag nice and roomy. I also like the fact that you can see a hint of the floral lining when you are carrying it.

Of course, you could make real curtains with this cross-stitch design as well. It is fun, though, to take a product like curtain tape and use it out of context. When you think about what a product does and not what it is supposed to be used for, you can discover a whole world of creative tools in sewing stores.

how to make the cross-stitch handbag

To make sure that the paper pattern for the bag pieces is symmetrical, draw only one of the curves at the lower corners in step 1, then fold the pattern in half and cut both curves at once.

materials

For a finished handbag measuring approximately 15in (37.5cm) wide by 15in (37.5cm) tall, you will need:

1yd (90cm) each of two 44in (112cm) wide cotton fabrics as follows—

A = solid color (ROWAN Shot Cotton SC47)
B = medium-scale floral (ROWAN *Arbour* L05DE)
1¹/₂yd (1.3m) of 2¹/₂in (6cm) wide curtain tape
Matching sewing thread
One skein of six-stranded cotton embroidery floss (ANCHOR light blue No. 1032)

stitching the handbag

1 To make a paper pattern for the handbag pieces, draw a rectangle 24¹/₂in by 16in (62cm by 40.5cm) on a large piece of paper and cut it out. Draw a curve at each bottom corner using a plate as a template, and trim off the corners.

2 Using the paper pattern, cut two pieces from fabric A (the solid-colored fabric) for the front and back, and two pieces from fabric B (the floral print) for the lining (see below).

3 Cut two 24¹/₂in (62cm) lengths of curtain tape. Pin and baste one piece to the wrong side of the front of the handbag, 1¹/₂in (4cm) below the top edge. Using a matching thread, machine stitch the tape in place, close to the top and bottom edges (see below). Stitch a length of tape to the back of the bag in the same way.

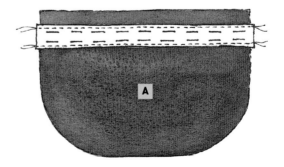

4 For each handle, cut a strip 26in by 4½in (66cm by 12cm) from fabric A and make two tubes of fabric (see page 28).

5 Baste a handle to the right side of the bag front, with each end 5in (13cm) from the side edge and the raw edges aligned with the top. Pin, baste, and machine stitch the lining to the front along the top edge, with the right sides together and leaving a ½in (1.5cm) seam allowance (see below). Remove the basting and press the seam open. Prepare the bag back in the same way.

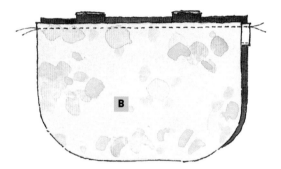

6 Gather the top of the bag front with the curtain tape so it measures 16in (40.5cm) wide. Knot the drawstrings to secure them. Adjust the gathers evenly and pin each gather to hold it in position. To secure the gathers, work cross-stitches on the right side of the front as shown (see below), using all six

strands of the cotton embroidery floss together. Gather then embroider the back of the bag in the same way.

7 Pin and baste the front of the bag to the back, with the right sides together. Be sure to match the seam lines carefully and avoid catching the handles. Machine stitch around the edge, leaving a small opening in the lining seam (see below).

8 Turn the bag right-side out, and slip stitch the opening in the lining closed. Then push the lining inside the bag. Machine or hand topstitch along the top edge of the bag to create a neat finish.

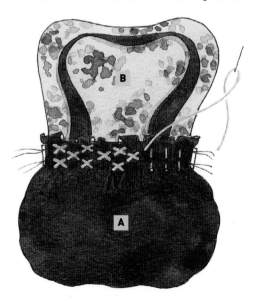

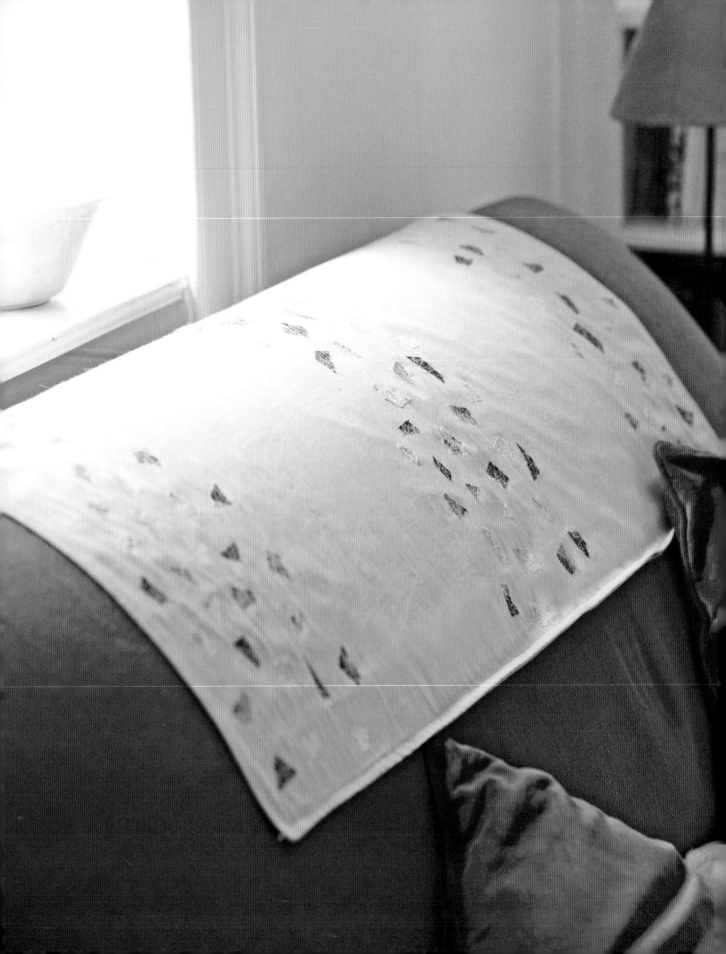

sofa throw

If you can't bear to throw away leftover scraps of your favorite fabrics, you probably have drawers full of tiny pieces like I do. Here is an embroidery technique that will use up at least a few precious remnants and showcase them beautifully. You simply fuse randomly cut patches onto the ground fabric, then machine embroider them with random lines of stitching.

The design possibilities of this fabric mosaic technique are endless. For example, the patches could be arranged to create the illusion that they are falling from the top, with a greater density of pieces at the bottom of the throw. Or an all-over pattern could be worked by grouping patches of the same or similar color into areas that form stripes, squares, or triangles.

This throw does not have to be used to cover the back of a sofa either—it would make an equally good pet blanket for a pampered pooch!

how to make the sofa throw

If you are using different fabrics than those specified below for the throw, make sure that the wool backing is not darker than the cotton front or it may show through.

materials

For a finished throw measuring approximately 44in by 30½in (112cm by 77cm), you will need:

1¼yd (120cm) of a 44in (112cm) wide ecru cotton fabric (ROWAN *Shot Cotton* SC24) for the front

1¼yd (120cm) of a 44in (112cm) wide pastel blue wool fabric for the backing

8in by 10in (20cm by 25cm) piece of each of at least four different floral/leaf cotton prints for the patches (ROWAN *Arbour* LO5DE, *Flower Sprays* LO1GD, *Dotted Leaf* LO3GN, and *Leaves* G30RD)

Paper-backed fusible bonding web adhesive

Ecru machine thread for sewing seams and for embroidery

preparing the throw ground fabric

1 Cut a 44in by 31½in (115cm by 80cm) rectangle from the ecru cotton fabric for the front of the throw. Cut a rectangle of the same size from the wool fabric for the back of the throw. These fabric rectangles for the back and front of the throw include a ½in (1.5cm) seam allowance around the edge of the two pieces. (You can make a bigger throw if you like, but be sure to purchase more patch fabric and prepare more patches in step 3 if you do so.)

2 Pin the cotton fabric rectangle on top of the wool fabric rectangle, with right sides together and the raw edges aligned. Baste then machine stitch all around the edges, leaving a ½in (1.5cm) seam allowance. Leave a small opening in the seam at one side of the throw for turning the throw right-side out (see below).

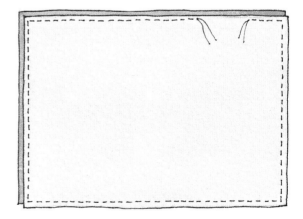

3 Once the seam is complete, remove the basting stitches. To ensure crisp corners on the finished sofa throw, clip off a small triangle of the seam allowance at each of the four corners, about ⅛in (3mm) from the seam. Then turn the throw right-side out by pulling it through the gap in the seam, and press carefully. Next, turn under the raw edges of the opening and pin. Topstitch around the edge of the throw, closing the opening as you do so.

machine-embroidering the throw

1 Fuse fusible bonding web adhesive to the wrong side of each of the fabric-print pieces, following the manufacturer's instructions. Do not remove the backing paper.

2 With the backing paper still in place, cut the fabric-print pieces into random shapes as shown below.

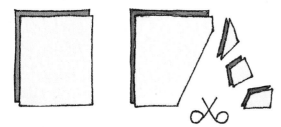

3 To mark panels for the positions of the embroidered patches, first place a pin at the lengthwise center at each side of the throw. Then mark three 8in (20cm) wide panels with basting stitches. Position one panel widthwise across the center and one at each end as shown below. As well as providing a guide for positioning the patches, these basted lines will keep the two layers firmly together when you begin the machine embroidery.

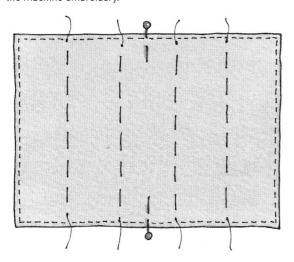

4 Arrange the randomly shaped patches inside the three marked sections on the throw front, peeling off the paper backing on each as you position them. Unless you have a huge

ironing table, it is easiest to do this one section at a time. Fuse the patches in place as you proceed (see below).

5 Once all the patches are fused in place, you can begin the machine embroidery. Put the darning presser foot on your sewing machine and disengage the feed dogs so the machine is ready for free-motion embroidery. Using an ecru thread, randomly free-motion machine stitch straight lines in all directions across each patch as shown below. It is not necessary to use an embroidery hoop for this embroidery as the wool backing fabric acts as a stabilizer.

6 Remove the basting and clip off the stray embroidery-thread ends. Press to finish.

embroidered flowers

These machine-embroidered flowers are truly handmade and do not pretend to be anything else. They look like magical cartoon flowers. Years ago, I used to make a variation of the petals using colored tights stretched over pliable wire, then bought a bunch that were made in a similar way but with fabric. The versions here are inspired by both these ideas and I have been meaning to make them for such a long time. As is so often the case with projects like this, when you finally find the time to sit down and create them, they give a wonderful sense of achievement, and every time you walk past them they lift your spirits.

There is no need to confine your embroidered flowers to a vase. Use a single flower to adorn a hair clip, or make a brooch by attaching a safety pin to the back of a short-stemmed version. You could even make one for a buttonhole on a special occasion.

Personalize the flowers by changing the fabrics, adding more petals, or even joining a few store-bought stamens into the centers. The world of flower making is exciting for the embroiderer, offering an original way of displaying machine-embroidery skills. Why not make some flower petals with no fabric at all, just purely machine lace, like the bowls on pages 90–95?

how to make the embroidered flowers

The flower petals are machine embroidered using free-motion machine stitches. If you are trying machine embroidery for the first time, it is best to read the detailed instructions on pages 24–27 and test your stitching on scrap fabric before beginning.

materials

For four different flowers, each with four 2in (5cm) long petals, you will need:
Small amount of each of four different floral/leaf prints (ROWAN *Vegetable Leaves* N05RD, Marigold N07YE, *Arbour* L05DE, and *Arbour* L05TO) for the petals, and of four different toning plain colors (ROWAN *Shot Cottons*) to back the flower petals
Paper-backed fusible bonding web adhesive
Thick, transparent, water-soluble vanishing fabric
Fabric adhesive spray for basting (optional)
Contrasting machine thread for embroidery
Matching thread for sewing petals together and binding buds to stems
Stiff florist's wire for the stems
Pliable florist's wire for anchoring the petals
Green florist's tape
Selection of small, colored glass beads for flower centers
Cotton wool for buds

machine embroidering the petals

1 Using the fusible bonding web and following the manufacturer's instructions, fuse a solid-colored fabric to the wrong side of each of the four prints. Each flower requires four petals, and the size of the fabric pieces depends on the number of flowers you are making. A 6½in (16.5cm) square is big enough for a single flower.

2 Trace the petal shape (see page 107), transfer it onto stiff, thin cardboard, and cut it out.

3 Using the cardboard template, trace four petals for each flower onto the backed fabric (see below), and cut them out.

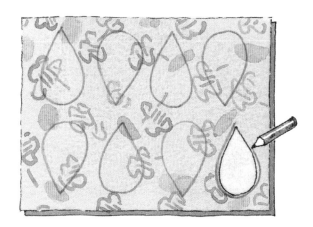

4 Baste or spray glue the petals to the right side of a piece of water-soluble vanishing fabric. Then lay another layer of water-soluble vanishing fabric on top of the petals to create a smooth surface for stitching. Stretch the layers in an embroidery hoop.

5 Put the darning presser foot on your sewing machine and disengage the feed dogs so the machine is ready for free-motion embroidery. Choose one of the three embroidery designs for each flower (see below). Using a contrasting

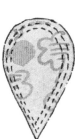

thread, free-motion machine stitch the petals (see below), remembering to use a single embroidery design for all four petals of each flower.

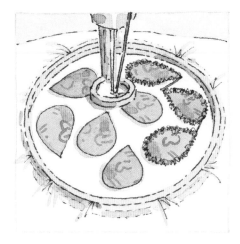

6 Once the embroidery is complete, cut away any stray threads. Remove the water-soluble fabric from the hoop and immerse the embroidered petals in water to dissolve the ground fabric. Take the petals out of the water while they are still fairly sticky so they will be slightly stiff when dry. Sandwich the damp petals between two pieces of scrap cloth, and press them to accelerate the drying process.

assembling the flowers

1 Hand stitch four matching petals together, using a matching thread and overlapping the petals at the tips (see below).

2 Hook a length of pliable florist's wire over the center of the flower and wind the two ends around a 8–12in (20–30cm) length of stiff florist's wire to form the stem (see above).

3 Wrap florist's tape all around the stem and up to the flower petals. Continue wrapping the tape as shown until the end tips of the petals are covered and they feel secure (see right). Leave a short piece of tape unwrapped—this will be used to cover the beading threads.

4 With the thread used for the embroidery, sew beads into the center of the flower. Start and finish the beading with a few tacking stitches into the machine embroidery, and stitch down and through the florist's tape (see right). Wrap the remaining length of tape around the top of the stem to cover the beading stitches.

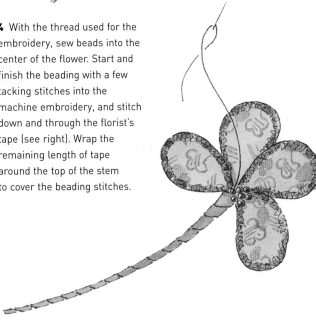

3 Roll up the fabric over the cotton wool to form the bud (see below).

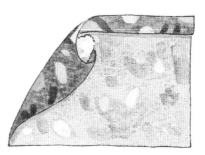

4 Stick a 8–12in (20–30cm) length of firm wire into the bud. Then wrap the end of the bud with matching thread to secure it firmly in place (see below).

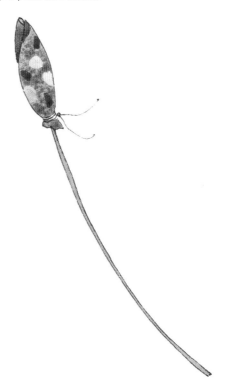

making the flower buds

1 For each bud, cut a rectangle of fabric 1¼in by 2in (3cm by 5cm). Fold under ¼in (6mm) along one long side and press.

2 Twist a small piece of cotton wool between your fingers to make a bud shape. Then place the cotton wool on the fabric as shown below.

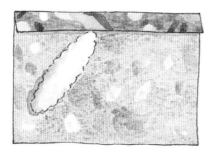

5 Wrap the stem and bottom of the bud with florist's tape as for the flowers (see page 59).

appliqué napkins

There is something quite genteel and, indeed, eco-friendly about the cloth napkin, but unfortunately, with the rise of the disposable variety it is becoming a rarity now.

Make these machine-appliquéd napkins to give your table setting a wonderful injection of color and a sense of occasion. If you like, you can stitch the appliqué onto readymade napkins to speed up the process. The advantage of making them from scratch, however, is that you can position the flowers closer to the corner because the unhemmed fabric gives you more room for the embroidery hoop.

The technique that I have used here leaves a raw edge around the appliqué and through constant washing the edge will fray slightly. If you prefer a crisper line, simply edge the flowers in satin stitch using a close machine zigzag stitch (see page 25).

how to make the appliqué napkins

Choose a single solid-colored fabric for the napkins, or make a multicolored set by varying the background color but using the same dot print for all the appliqué.

materials

For a set of four finished napkins, each measuring approximately 14½in by 14½in (37cm by 37cm), you will need:
Two 44in (112cm) wide cotton fabrics as follows—
  A = 1yd (90cm) of a solid color (ROWAN *Shot Cotton* in, for example, SC09, SC15, SC21, or SC41)
  B = ¼yd (25cm) of a medium-scale dot print (ROWAN *Batik Confetti* BKC05)
Paper-backed fusible bonding web adhesive
8in (20cm) embroidery hoop
Contrasting machine thread for embroidery
Matching thread for hemming

stitching the napkin

1 For each napkin, cut a square 16in by 16in (41cm by 41cm) from fabric A (the solid-colored fabric).

2 For the appliqué for each napkin, cut a square approximately 5in by 5in (13cm by 13cm) from fabric B (the medium-scale dot print). Cut a piece of fusible bonding web to the same size, and fuse it to the wrong side of the fabric following the manufacturer's instructions. Leave the paper backing in place.

3 Trace the petal and flower-center shapes (see page 106), transfer them onto stiff, thin cardboard, and cut them out.

4 Using the cardboard templates, trace six petals and one center for each napkin onto the paper stuck to the back of fabric B (see below).

5 Cut out the appliqué pieces and peel off the paper backings. Then position the petals and the flower center adhesive-side down at the corner of each napkin, with the outer points at least 1¼in (3cm) from the raw side edges (see below). Fuse the petals in place.

6 Put the darning presser foot on your machine and disengage the feed dogs so the machine is ready for free-motion embroidery. Stretch the napkin in an embroidery hoop, centering the flower. Free-motion machine stitch the appliqué in place close to the edges. Add two more lines of stitching around the petals to accentuate the shapes (see below and bottom right). Take the fabric out of the hoop and press.

7 To hem the edges of the napkin, first fold under ¼in (5mm) all around the raw edges. Then turn under ½in (1.5cm), pinning as you proceed (see below). Baste the hem in place and machine topstitch close to the first fold. Remove the basting and press.

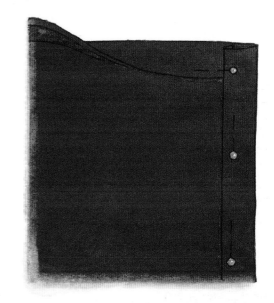

table runner

This table runner was designed to coordinate with the napkins on page 62. The basic, easy-to-stitch machine embroidery creates a bold design that works especially well if made in starkly contrasting colors. The strong ground and white embroidery thread make a great backdrop for table settings. If you prefer, you can reverse the bicolor scheme, working the flowers in a dark thread on a light-toned fabric.

The embroidered flowers are much easier to machine stitch than they look. First, you trace the flower outlines onto the runner fabric at random using templates. Then you stitch, following the outlines loosely and filling in the larger flowers with additional petal shapes. Each flower ends up slightly different than the next, giving the runner a charming handmade look.

This is a format easy to adapt to any simple embroidery motif, figurative or geometric. You could even draw shapes freehand onto the fabric with a tailor's chalk pencil and stitch them in a jiffy.

how to make the table runner

The randomly positioned flowers on this runner are made with one, two, or three lines of stitching. Use the inner, center, or outside lines of the stitching for the different sizes of flower (see template on page 107).

materials

For a finished table runner measuring approximately 42¹/₂in by 10¹/₄in (108cm by 26cm), you will need:
¹/₂yd (45cm) of a solid-colored 44in (112cm) wide cotton cotton fabric (ROWAN *Shot Cotton* SC09)
8in (20cm) embroidery hoop
Thick white sewing thread for embroidery
Matching thread for hemming

stitching the table runner

1 To make templates for the flower embroidery, trace the three sizes of flower (see below) from page 107. Then transfer the flower shapes onto stiff, thin cardboard, and cut them out.

2 For the runner, cut a rectangle 44in by 11³/₄in (112cm by 30cm) from the solid-colored fabric of your choice (see Materials list for the shade used here).

3 Using the cardboard templates and a tailor's chalk pencil, trace the flower shapes onto the runner fabric (see below). Position the various flower sizes at random intervals along the lengthwise center of the fabric, keeping them at least 3¹/₄in (8cm) from the raw edges of the fabric.

4 Put the darning presser foot on your machine and disengage the feed dogs so the machine is ready for free-motion machine embroidery. Stretch one of the outlined flowers in an embroidery hoop. Using thick white thread, embroider the flower (see below); follow the chalk line for the outer outline and fill in the inner lines on the two larger flowers freehand. Work each flower in the same way. Press the finished embroidery.

5 To hem the edges of the runner, first fold under and press ¼in (5mm) all around the raw edges. Then turn under ½in (1.5cm), pinning as you proceed (see below). Baste the hem in place. Using a matching machine thread, machine topstitch the hem in place close to the first fold. Remove the basting and press.

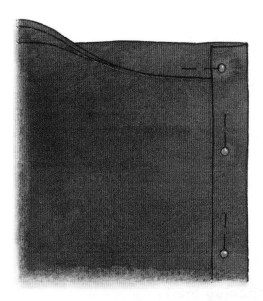

large flowers

The large flowers on the table runner can be stitched in a continuous line if you like. Start at the center of the motif and stitch outward along the edge of one of the large petals. Turn at the tip of the petal and stitch to the center. Then continue outward around the opposite petal in a figure-eight path. Continue like this working all the outer then inner petals in figure eights. End the stitching at the center.

purse

I really wanted to experiment with an all-over hand-embroidered design, and these purses wear it well. Working onto a fabric print is a wonderful way of creating a feeling of complex detail without actually doing that much work. Choose colors carefully and you will enhance the print and produce an entirely different fabric; choose the wrong color and the embroidery will sink into obscurity. The key is to choose fairly simple prints with blocks of space that are begging to be decorated. Then to embroider, select a color that appears in small quantities within the print.

Little purses are always incredibly useful. Use them when you don't want to lug a wallet full of credit cards around all the time, or simply to add fun and color to your handbag. This purse would make a lovely first purse for a child. Remember, though, that when you give purses as presents, you should always put a penny inside for good luck—at least that's what my grandmother told me.

how to make the purse

If you want to duplicate the colorway below, use the first shade numbers given in the Materials list. For the colorway on page 70, use the second shade numbers.

materials

For each finished purse measuring approximately 5¾in by 3¾in (14.5cm by 9.5cm), you will need:

¼yd (25cm) of each of two 44in (112cm) wide cotton fabrics as follows—

A = large-scale circles print (ROWAN *Spools* G34MG or G34JA)

B = solid color (ROWAN *Shot Cotton* SC09 or SC27)

Two skeins of six-stranded cotton embroidery floss (ANCHOR tangerine No. 304 or red No. 335)

6in (15cm) zipper (pink or red)

Heavy-weight interfacing

8in (20cm) embroidery hoop

Matching thread

hand embroidering the purse

1 Cut a 10in (25cm) square from fabric A. Using a water-soluble pen, draw the purse outline at the center—a rectangle 5¾in (14.5cm) wide by 3¾in (9.5cm) tall. Then draw the seam allowance ½in (1.5cm) from the first outline (see below).

2 Stretch the marked purse front in an embroidery hoop, centering the design. Then thread a needle with a length of all six strands of the embroidery floss and knot the thread at one end. Embroider the purse front,

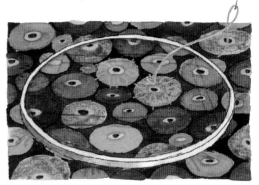

using lazy daisy stitches to form flowers within the larger circles of the print (see below). Embroider flowers at random within the purse outline, avoiding working into the corners too closely. You can embroider over the drawn seam line, but do not embroider over the outer cutting line or your embroidery will unravel when the front piece is trimmed.

3 Once the embroidery is complete, remove the purse front from the hoop and press.

4 Trim the purse front to the edge of the marked seam allowance. Using the front as a template, cut one back piece, two lining pieces, and two interfacing pieces.

5 Baste the interfacing to the front and back of the purse, stitching around the sides and bottom of each piece. Then turn under ¹/₂in (1.5cm) along the top edge on both pieces and press. Pin the zipper in place between the folded edges and baste (see below). The folded edges should meet, concealing the zipper teeth. Machine stitch the zipper in place, using a zipper foot and matching thread.

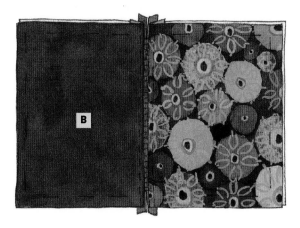

6 Fold the purse right sides together, leaving the zipper slightly open. Pin then baste around the sides and bottom. Using a water-soluble pen, draw the seam line on one side of the purse. Position the seam line ¹/₂in (1.5cm) from the sides and bottom, curve it at the corners (you can use a CD as a template), and taper it a little at the top edges to meet the zipper (see below).

7 Machine stitch the front and back together along the marked seam line. Trim the seam allowances to ¹/₄in (6mm) and carefully remove any remaining basting. (Do not turn right-side out yet.)

8 Using the purse as a template, trim the lining pieces to the same shape at the sides and bottom corners, but leave the hem allowance at the top. With right sides together, pin the two lining pieces to each other and stitch around the sides and bottom, leaving a ¹/₄in (6mm) seam allowance. Turn the lining right-side out and slip it over the purse. Turn under the hem at the top and slip stitch the lining to the purse (see below). Turn the purse right-side out.

lampshade

Sometimes the simplest hand embroidery can be used to great decorative effect, a fact that is often forgotten. As a result, I was determined to create a project for this book that used only simple lines of running stitch. There is so much scope for design with this most basic of stitches. You could use it, as I have done, to form stripes or make checks, or use it as an outline for a motif. On top of this, you could experiment with textured thread, color combinations, and length of stitch.

Readymade lampshades are available in all sizes, colors, and shapes, so you should easily be able to tailor this project to suit any setting.

One thing to remember is that light will shine through any holes made with the needle when the lamp is on. For this reason, I suggest marking the stitching lines before beginning to avoid mistakes.

how to make the lampshade

When hand embroidering a lampshade, with each stitch you will need to pass the needle from one hand on the outside of the shade to the other hand inside the shade, so choose the readymade lampshade carefully. It should be sturdy enough to take the stitching and big enough for you to reach one hand inside to make the stitches with ease.

materials

For a lampshade of the desired size, you will need:
Readymade lampshade, in red or chosen color
Two skeins of each of two colors of six-stranded cotton
    embroidery floss (ANCHOR green No. 255 and tangerine
    No. 304 or two chosen colors)
Self-adhesive ribbon to cover the inside edges of the
    lampshade

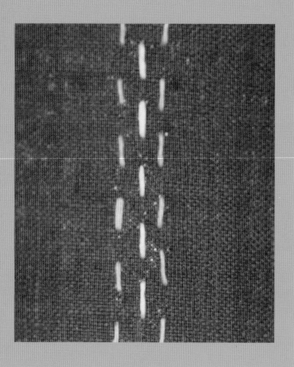

hand embroidering the lampshade

1 To mark the positions of the embroidery lines, first measure the top and bottom circumferences of your lampshade. Then divide each measurement by eight. Use these calculated numbers to mark eight equidistant points around the top and bottom edges of the lampshade, using a tailor's chalk pencil (see below). (Most lampshades have a seam running from the top edge down to the bottom edge and this is a good place for the first mark.) Draw vertical lines joining the top and bottom marks—these are the guidelines for the hand embroidery.

2 Thread a needle with a length of all six strands of the color of cotton embroidery floss you are using for the central line of stitching in the vertical bands of stitches (green was used on this version). Knot the end of the thread. Work long, bold running stitches along each of the eight marked vertical lines (see below), finishing each line of stitches with another knot. Make sure the length of embroidery floss is long enough for a whole line to avoid running out of thread in the middle.

4 Neaten the inside of the lampshade by carefully sticking self-adhesive ribbon to the inside top and bottom edges of the shade (see below). This not only disguises the tail ends of the embroidery threads, but also secures them firmly in place.

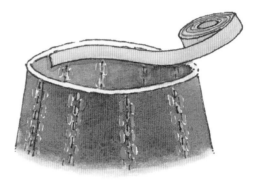

alternative stitching designs

If you like, experiment with alternative designs for your lampshade. Test thread colors on a fabric the same color as the lampshade, and try out long and short stitches.

3 Using the second color of embroidery floss, work a vertical line of running stitch on each side of each of the central lines already worked (see below). Position these lines about ¹⁄₂in (12mm) from the central line.

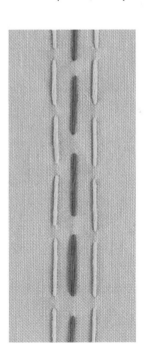
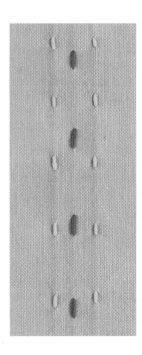

appliqué cushions

These cushions are very bright, but I love using fabrics in unusual and unexpected ways. Creating combinations like this—plain, naïve flowers on an intense floral ground—is part of the fun of embroidery. If you want a sofa full of vibrant cushions, try making some cushions that work the other way around, with the plain fabric as the background and the floral as the petals.

The machine satin stitch works a treat here to accentuate the flowers, but you can also machine embroider petals using a simple straight stitch. Leaving raw edges on the appliqué does mean that there will be some fraying over time, but the slight air of shabby chic has its charm.

You can make these cushions in any floral fabric, just make sure that the color you pick for the appliqué is a minor color in the print. They do not have to be this bright either. If you were to choose more muted tones, the design would work equally well.

how to make the appliqué cushions

The cushion with the single-flower appliqué has a single large yellow flower with seven petals. The alternative cushion has four smaller blue flowers, each with six smaller petals. The same background print is used for each cushion, although the flower color differs.

materials

For each finished cushion measuring approximately 14in (35cm) square, you will need:

Two 44in (112cm) wide cotton fabrics as follows—
   A = ¹/₂yd (45cm) of a large-scale floral/vegetable print (ROWAN *Cabbages and Roses* G38WN)
   B = ¹/₄yd (25cm) of a solid color (ROWAN *Shot Cotton* SC11 or SC41)
Paper-backed fusible bonding web adhesive
Matching machine thread for embroidering appliqué
Small embroidery hoop
Matching thread for sewing cushion
Pillow form, 14in (35cm) square

working the machine appliqué

1 For the front of the cushion, cut a square 15in by 15in (38cm by 38cm) from fabric A (the large-scale print).

2 For the appliqué, cut a piece 20in by 8in (50cm by 20cm) from fabric B (the solid-colored fabric). Cut a piece of fusible bonding web to the same size and fuse it to the wrong side of the fabric following the manufacturer's instructions (for successful results, always follow the manufacturer's advise for the iron temperature). Leave the paper backing in place.

3 Trace the appropriate petal size (see page 106) for your chosen cushion design, transfer it onto stiff, thin cardboard, and cut it out.

4 Using the chosen template, trace seven large petals or 24 small petals onto the fusible-bonding-web paper (see below).

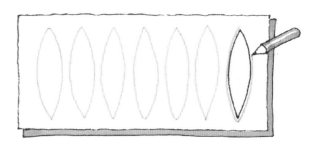

5 Cut out the petals and peel off the paper backings. Then position the petals on the cushion front (see below). To center the large flower, first fold the fabric into quarters and mark the center point with a pin or tailor's chalk. Position the four small six-petal flowers at random. Be sure to leave room at the center of all the flowers for the machine-embroidered flower-center circle. Fuse the petals in place.

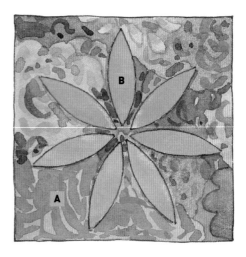

6 Put the general-purpose presser foot on your sewing machine and set the machine for the widest, most closely spaced zigzag stitch (machine satin stitch). Using a matching thread, zigzag stitch around each petal, starting and finishing at the point at the center of the flower (see below). See page 25 for more information on zigzag stitching and how to turn the corners on the petals. Once you have finished edging all the petals, press the front.

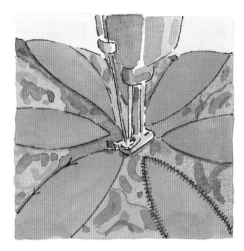

7 Put the darning presser foot on your machine and disengage the feed dogs, so the machine is ready for free-motion machine embroidery. Stretch the cushion front in an embroidery hoop with a flower center in the middle. Free-motion machine stitch a dense circle of machine embroidery in the center of each flower. Take the cushion front out of the hoop and press.

sewing on the cushion back

1 For the cushion-cover back, cut out two rectangles each 15in by 10½in (38cm by 26.5cm) from fabric A.

2 Turn under ½in (1.5cm) along one long edge of each rectangle to form a hem and press. Pin each hem in position and machine stitch. Overlap the two back pieces by 5in (12cm) so that they form a single piece the same size as the cushion front, and pin them together.

3 Pin and baste the cushion back pieces to the appliquéd front, with the right sides together. Machine stitch, leaving a ½in (1.5cm) seam allowance (see below). Remove the basting.

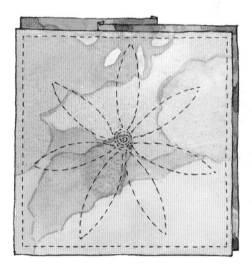

4 To ensure crisp corners, clip off a triangle of the seam allowance at each of the four corners before turning the cover right-side out. To do this, cut diagonally across the corner about ⅛in (3mm) from the seam. Turn the cushion cover right-side out and insert the pillow form.

glasses case

Too many of us make do with really dull or cumbersome glasses cases, and sometimes with no case at all. I decided it was time to design a pretty, safe haven for glasses, and came up with this simple solution. You only need scraps of fabric to make this case and the most basic hand-embroidery skill. The simple contrasting blanket-stitch edging is decorative as well as functional.

Be sure to add a small snap fastener to the top opening for very slim glasses that may slip out. If your glasses are of the large Jackie O variety, add a little extra width to the initial rectangles when cutting out the fabric pieces.

You can personalize the glasses case by using a color combination of your choice. Alternatively, add simple embroidery to the fabric pieces, or quilt them before stitching the back and front together (see the purses on pages 70 and 72 and the chair-seat pad on page 33).

how to make the glasses case

Use your own choice of fabrics or one of the two combinations of Rowan fabrics in the Materials list. For the colorway below, use the first shade numbers given below. For the version on page 83, use the second shade numbers given (this colorway has a stripe on the outside and a floral print on the inside).

materials

For a finished glasses case measuring approximately 8in by 3³⁄₄in (20cm by 9cm), you will need:
Small amount of each of two cotton fabrics as follows—
A = medium-scale floral or stripe (ROWAN *Marigold* N07RD or *Awning Stripe* AWS01)
B = solid color or small-scale floral (ROWAN *Shot Cotton* SC17 or *Flower Sprays* LO1TA) for lining
Lightweight batting
One skein of six-stranded cotton embroidery floss (ANCHOR hot pink No. 54 or light turquoise No. 185)
Snap (optional)

stitching the glasses case

1 First, make paper patterns for the two glasses case pieces. Draw a rectangle 9in by 4³⁄₄in (23cm by 12cm) for the back of the case and a rectangle 8¹⁄₄in by 4³⁄₄in (21cm by 12cm) for the front. Cut out these paper rectangles. Then draw rounded edges at each of the four corners of each rectangle, using a CD as a template (see below). Carefully trim off the corners. These paper patterns include the ¹⁄₂in (1.5cm) seam allowances. (Test the paper patterns on your glasses and redraw the pieces if necessary, adding extra width or length as required.)

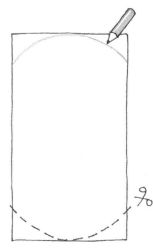

2 Using the paper pattern for the back of the glasses case, cut a piece from fabric A (the medium-scale floral fabric or the stripe); a piece from fabric B (the solid-colored fabric or the floral) for the lining; and a piece from the batting. Using the paper pattern for the front of the glasses case, cut the same three layers.

3 Pin together the three layers for the back of the case with the batting on the bottom, the lining right-side up in the middle, and the outer fabric wrong-side up on top. Baste then machine stitch the layers together, leaving a 1/2in (1.5cm) seam allowance and leaving an opening in the seam at one side for turning right-side out (see below). Stitch the layers for the front of the case together in the same way. Trim the seam allowances on each piece to 1/4in (6mm).

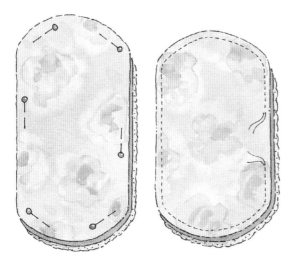

4 Turn the back and the front pieces right-side out so the lining and outer fabric are on the outside and the batting in between. Press. Sew the openings closed with a ladder stitch (see below).

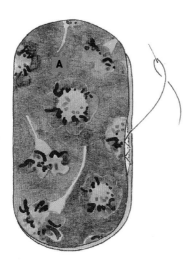

5 Place the shorter prepared front piece on top of the prepared back piece, with the wrong sides together. Make sure all the sides are aligned, then baste the back and front together along the sides and bottom, leaving the top open. Using a length of all six strands of the cotton embroidery floss, blanket stitch the front and back together (see below). When working the blanket stitch, position the looped edge of the stitch on top of the fabric rather than along the edge of the pieces in the usual way. Secure the stitching at each end with a few extra stitches.

6 If desired, stitch a snap to the lining of the glasses case just below the top edge (see below).

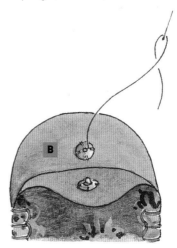

cutwork doilies

Over the years, I have collected a large number of vintage doilies, and although I could never imagine recreating any of them, they are a great source of inspiration. They were originally used to protect and decorate surfaces all around the home, placed underneath potted plants and ornaments. I wanted to design modern versions that would be vibrant in color and design, yet still have a slight air of nostalgia. I used the simple technique of machine embroidering around the edges of the cut-out printed flowers to imitate cutwork embroidery.

These modern doilies contain two secret ingredients. The first, fusible bonding web, is an adhesive used to bond two layers of fabric together to create a "new" heavier-weight fabric. The other ingredient is water-soluble vanishing fabric, which provides a temporary sturdy surface for stitching on the flower motifs.

Of course, you can make the doily any size. If small doilies are just too old-fashioned for you, make a set to use as coasters, or make bigger ones for place mats.

how to make the cutwork doilies

The two variations shown on page 86 and below are made from a single colorway of Rowan *Flowers* fabric, using the tangerine/brown flowers for the doily on page 86 and the purple/green flowers for the doily below. The center fabric for each doily uses a plain toning cotton.

materials

For a finished doily measuring approximately 10in (25cm) in diameter, you will need:

Two 44in (112cm) wide cotton fabrics as follows—

A = small amount of a solid color (ROWAN *Shot Cotton* SC11 tangerine or *Shot Cotton* SC39 apple)

B = ¹/₂yd (45cm) of a large-scale floral print (ROWAN *Flowers* GR1AN)

Paper-backed fusible bonding web adhesive

Fabric adhesive spray for basting (optional)

Contrasting machine thread for embroidery

Water-soluble vanishing fabric, 12in (30cm) square

machine embroidering the doilies

1 Cut two pieces of fabric A (the solid-colored fabric) and one piece of fusible bonding web, each 8in by 8in (23cm by 23cm). Fuse the two pieces of fabric A together following the manufacturer's instructions (see below).

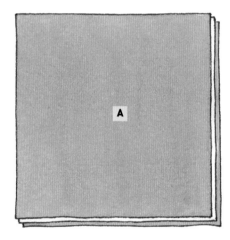

2 Repeat step 1, but using fabric B (the floral fabric) for one of the fabric pieces and backing it with a piece of fabric A (see below). Make sure there are at least seven full flower blooms on fabric B.

3 Cut out the seven flowers (see right). Form them in a ring to determine the size of the center circle of the mat— the flowers should slightly overlap each other and the center circle. Draw the center on the plain fabric using a bowl or glass as a template, and cut it out.

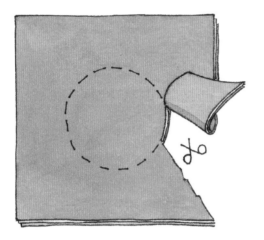

4 Lay the fabric center right-side up on a piece of water-soluble fabric. Arrange the flowers around the center so that they very slightly overlap each other and the center circle. Pin then baste the pieces in place (see below), or use fabric adhesive spray.

5 Put the general-purpose presser foot on your sewing machine and set the machine for a wide, close zigzag stitch (machine satin stitch). Zigzag stitch over the exposed raw edges of the center circle (see above).

6 Edge each of the flowers with close zigzag stitch in the same way (see below). Cut away the excess water-soluble fabric around the edge of the mat and rinse away the rest. Leave to dry, then press.

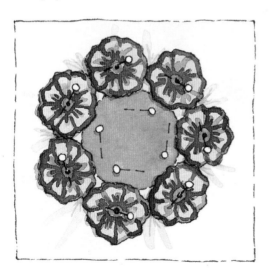

machine-lace bowl

I love using water-soluble vanishing fabric; it is like a secret ingredient in an embroiderer's recipe book. Anyone not aware of its invention will be baffled as to how you achieved such a web of threads—the results look much more time-consuming than they actually are. The coating of the dissolving fabric left on the threads makes the bowl hold the shape of the mold when dry.

I have seen so many variations of the embroidered bowl, most heavily laden with texture and color. While these are very beautiful and intricate, I thought it would be interesting to show a really pared-down version in a single color. The bowl is not fantastically practical, but it does make an elegant decorative piece, the emphasis firmly laid on the lace formations of the stitch.

It is entirely up to you whether you choose to stick with the minimal or experiment with the highly decorative ideas that could lead on from here. You can sandwich whatever you like between the layers of dissolvable fabric as long as it will not break the machine needle; feathers, sequins, ribbons, and textured threads could all work well, and when the bowl is finished you can continue with hand stitches and beads.

how to make the machine-lace bowl

The stitching looks very different when the vanishing fabric is rinsed out, so it is a good idea to try out a small swatch before starting your bowl.

materials

For a finished bowl measuring approximately 8in (20cm) in diameter and 2³/₄in (7cm) tall, you will need:
250yd (230m) of sewing thread in desired color
Thick, transparent, water-soluble vanishing fabric, 18in by 36in (46cm by 92cm)
Textured threads, ribbon, sequins, and feathers (optional)
Embroidery hoop
Round glass or ceramic bowl about 8in (20cm) in diameter and 2³/₄in (7cm) tall for the mold, and plastic wrap

machine stitching the bowl

1 Fold the water-soluble fabric in half widthwise. Measure your bowl mold from the the top edge across the bottom to the top edge, and draw a circle with this diameter on the folded fabric with a water-soluble pen (see below).

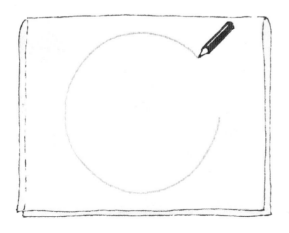

2 If you want to embellish the bowl, at this point insert textured threads, ribbon, sequins, and/or feathers between the two layers of water-soluble fabric. Baste around the circle circumference to keep the layers firmly together.

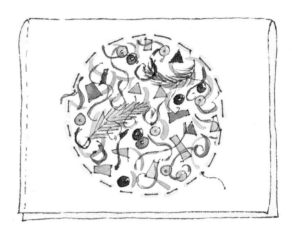

3 Stretch the water-soluble fabric in an embroidery hoop. Put the darning presser foot on your sewing machine and disengage the feed dogs, so the machine is ready for free-motion embroidery. Free-motion machine stitch swirls inside the drawn circle until the circle is a mass of stitches—the more stitches the denser the lace. (Make sure the stitched swirls are all interconnected or the lace will fall apart.)

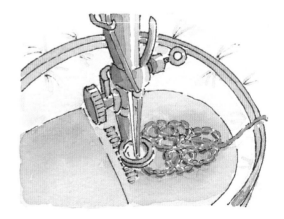

4 Once you have completed the stitching, take the work out of the hoop and cut away the excess water-soluble fabric around the outside of the circle. Immerse the stitched fabric in water and dissolve it until all that is left are very sticky stitches. (Do not dissolve the fabric completely; the stitches must remain sticky so the bowl is stiff when dry.) Put plastic film over the bowl mold and place the damp lace over it (see right). Once the bowl is dry, remove it with the aid of a blunt knife.

alternative bowls

I made several versions of the bowl, all using different stitching patterns. The white one is rather elegant (see below), and the embellished one great fun to compose (see next page).

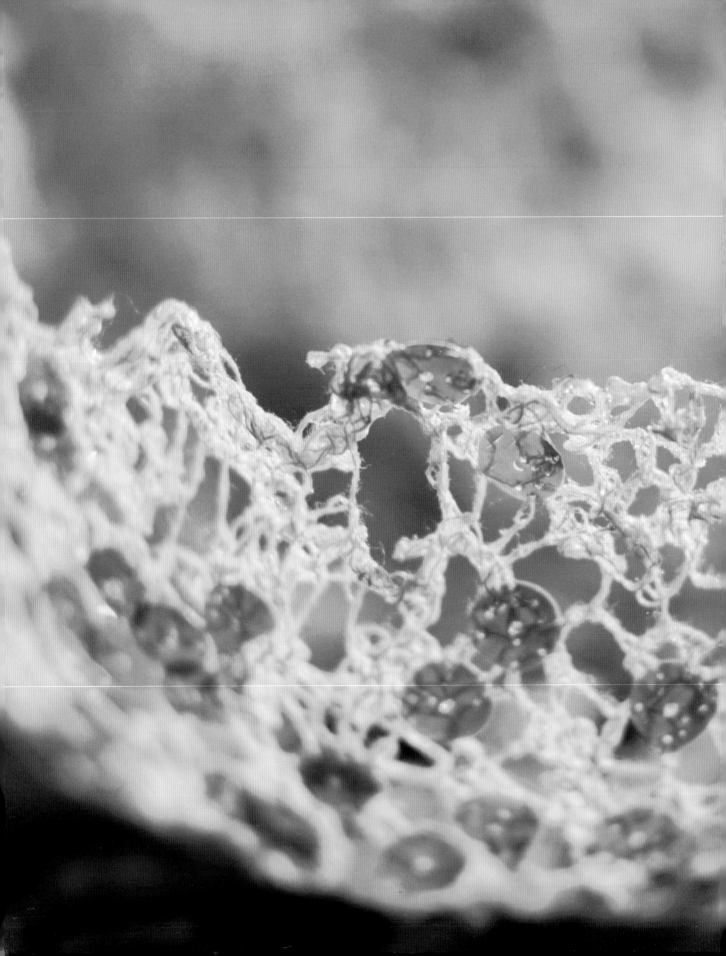

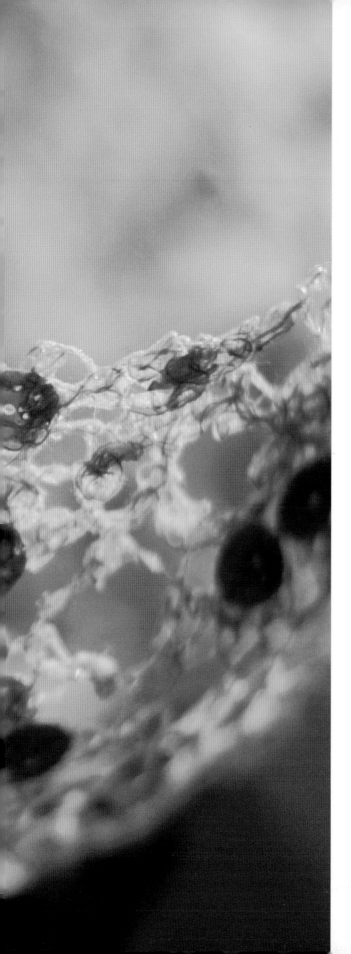

alternative bowl

This alternative design incorporates sequins, which add glittery highlights to the cotton-thread embroidery. It illustrates how you can add other decorative items to the lace bowl for interesting and unusual looks. To add things like sequins, feathers, or scraps of fabric or ribbon, place the decorative additions between two layers of thick, transparent, water-soluble fabric before beginning the stitching. Ensure that the machine-embroidery stitches are dense and interlinking so that they catch each decorative addition. If you want to add beads, stitch them onto the completed bowl.

check cards

I have to confess that I am not the best card sender in the world, but I love to receive them. Homemade ones are much more special and personal than store-bought.

Creating entire fabrics from scraps of old ones is really satisfying, and this project introduces you to just such a technique. This first stage is machine embroidering thin strips of fabric together. If you stop here, the result is a homemade stripe. If you go on to the final stage by cutting the stripes and stitching them together again, you will create a check effect like the one on these card designs. You could cut the stripes on the diagonal for yet another patched pattern.

Design possibilities are limitless. Vary the widths of the fabric strips for irregular checks, or use different machine or hand stitches for joining them. The list goes on and on.

Sit at your sewing machine with a box full of fabric scraps and experiment with these techniques—you will have a whole range of samples in no time at all. The most important thing to remember is that the more you cut and sew the fabric, the more it shrinks in size. Keep a pad of watercolor paper and some really pretty envelopes at the ready, so you can begin to build up a store of wonderful cards for every occasion.

how to make the check cards

The fabrics listed in the Materials below are for the machine-embroidered heart patchwork on page 97. To personalize your cards, use your own scraps.

materials

For a finished card approximately 4⅛in by 3in (10.5cm by 7cm), you will need:
Piece of watercolor paper, 8¼in by 6in (21cm by 14cm)
Small amount of at least four different cotton fabrics as follows—
    Solid color (ROWAN *Shot Cotton* SC07)
    Ikat stripe (ROWAN *Single Ikat* SIF06)
    Stripe (ROWAN *Twig Stripe* N03RD)
    Small-scale fruit/floral print (ROWAN *Fruits and Florals* N08RD)
Complementary machine thread for embroidery
Spray glue

stitching the card motifs

1 Using a craft knife and a metal ruler, carefully score the piece of watercolor paper widthwise through the center. (Make sure that the blade does not go through the paper; the aim is to score it lightly to facilitate a neat fold.) Fold the card along the scored line. Use this prepared card base to determine the size of your motif in step 5.

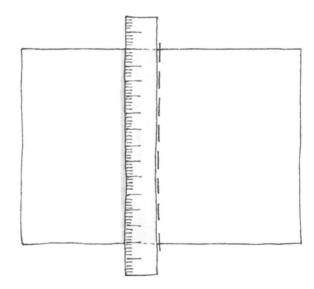

2 Cut at least two strips 1in (3cm) wide by 9in (22.5cm) long from each of the four fabrics (see below). (If you want to make more than one patched motif from your checkered patchwork or a motif for a larger card, then cut more strips or longer strips to make a bigger piece.)

3 Put the general-purpose presser foot on your sewing machine and set the machine for a wide, slightly spaced apart zigzag stitch (a medium stitch length). Overlap two different fabric strips lengthwise by ½in (1.5cm) and machine zigzag stitch them together, stitching over the raw edge. There is no need to pin or baste the strips together before stitching, as slight imperfections will only add to the charm of the finished patchwork. Continue overlapping the strips one at a time and machine zigzag stitching them in place as before (see below).

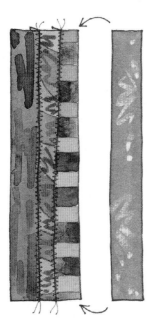

4 Once all the strips are joined on, press. Then cut 1in (2.5cm) strips from the patched piece, cutting in the opposite direction to the stitched lines (see below).

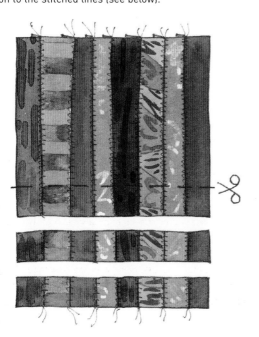

5 Staggering the positions of the fabrics to create a check effect, overlap the newly cut strips and zigzag stitch them together as before (see below). Cut the desired shape from the machine-embroidered patchwork—this could be an oblong rectangle, a heart, a star, etc.

6 Machine zigzag stitch around the shape to finish the raw edge (see below).

7 Spray the back of the patchwork with spray glue and stick it to the front of the prepared card.

hot water bottle cover

I don't know whether it's true to say that the technique used in this pattern can be called embroidery. It is more of a fabric manipulation, which I came across while researching my patchwork book. The technique transforms cotton into a luxurious pile fabric and is incredibly simple to work. The secret is to cut the lines on the bias so that the layers of fabric fray correctly. There are many special tools available to simplify the slashing process, but you could just as well use sharp scissors.

This hot water bottle cover uses only one fabric for the layers and an ikat print for the top. Because you can layer all sorts of prints and colors together and not have a clue what the finished effect will be, make a sample swatch before you begin. A lot of fabric is needed, so mistakes can be costly and disappointing, especially if just rearranging the layers would have created a much better effect.

Whole books have been written on this technique and it is certainly addictive. Try varying the lines of stitching or adding cut-out motifs to the top layers—these will be secured by the stitching. Finally, don't use thick batting; you will be surprised just how thick your finished fabric is.

how to make the hot water bottle cover

If you want to use this technique to make a small throw, cut the backing layer to a larger size than the top layers and use the excess to bind the edges (see page 29).

materials

For a finished hot water bottle cover to fit a standard hot water bottle, you will need:

Hot water bottle
Two 44in (112cm) wide cotton fabrics as follows—
A = ¹/₂yd (45cm) of a polka dot print (ROWAN *Double Ikat Polka Dot* DIP03)
B = 1³/₄yd (1.5m) of a solid color (ROWAN *Shot Cotton* SC07)
Lightweight batting, 18in by 30in (45cm by 76cm)
Fabric adhesive spray
Matching machine thread for the quilting

stitching the cover

1 First, make three paper pattern pieces for the cover. For the pattern for the cover front, lay the hot water bottle on a large piece of paper and trace around it (see below). Then add another outline 1in (2.5cm) around the first. Cut out this

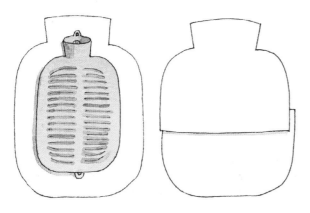

template. For the paper pattern for the two back pieces, trace the pattern just made onto a piece of paper and cut out the shape. Cut this new template in half widthwise and retrace each piece. Add 2in (5cm) to the center edge of each back piece for the final shapes, and cut out.

2 Using the paper pattern pieces prepared in step 1 and a water-soluble pencil, draw the three shapes onto separate rectangles of fabric A (dot print), allowing at least 1in (2.5cm) extra all around the shapes. Then cut out one rectangle of a lightweight batting and five of fabric B (solid color) to the same size as each of the three rectangles of fabric A. It is best to cut what will become the bottom layer of the top stack of

solid-colored fabric slightly larger than the rest, so that when you are slashing the top layers, the bottom layer is easy to identify. Use the fabric adhesive spray to baste the layers of each of the three groups together. With all the layers face up, position one layer of fabric B on the bottom for the lining, followed by the layer of batting, the largest layer of the solid colored fabric, the remaining layers of the solid-colored fabric, and lastly the dot print on top (see above).

3 Mark a diagonal line across the center of each rectangular stack with a water-soluble pen (see below).

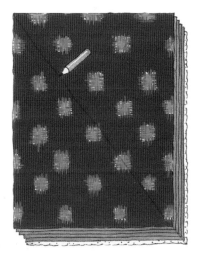

4 Put the walking presser foot on your sewing machine and machine stitch the layers of each stack together along the central diagonal line. Continue adding straight lines of machine stitching on alternate sides of the first line, parallel to it and about 1/2in (1.5cm) apart, until each rectangle is covered with diagonal lines (see below).

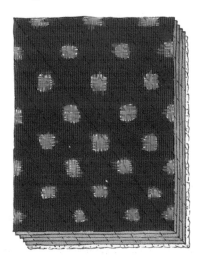

5 Once the diagonal lines of stitching are complete, slash the top four layers of fabric down the center between the lines of stitching, leaving intact the bottom layer of the solid-colored

fabric, the batting, and the lining layer (see below). Be sure to use a very sharp pair of scissors.

6 Using the paper patterns, trace the shapes on the lining side and cut them out. Turn under 1/2in (1.5cm) along center edges of the two back pieces, then pin, baste, and topstitch.

7 Pin and baste the front to the backs, with the right sides together and the two backs overlapping. Machine stitch, leaving a 1/2in (1.5cm) seam allowance. Trim the seam allowances and clip the curved seam allowances at the neck. Remove the basting and turn the cover right-side out.

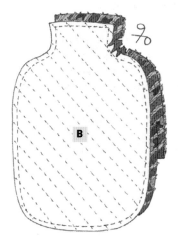

8 Create the chenille effect by washing the finished cover to make the cut edges fray. To fluff up the chenille-style edges even more, dry the cover in the dryer.

useful terms

*Backstitch Series of small hand stitches in which the thread is taken back over the stitch just made to create strong seams.

Basting Long running stitches used to hold two pieces of fabric together temporarily before they are machine stitched together.

Bias In fabric terminology, the 45-degree angle to the straight grain. Fabrics cut on the bias (i.e., at this angle) are stretchy.

Bias binding Strips of bias-cut fabrics used for border edgings because they will stretch around corners.

Darning foot Special circular sewing-machine foot used for free-motion machine embroidery or quilting.

Feed dogs The teeth under the throat plate of a sewing machine. They grip and move the fabric as it is stitched.

Free-motion machine embroidery Machine embroidery that is worked with the feed dogs disengaged so that you can move the fabric freely under the machine needle to create the desired stitches.

Fusible bonding web adhesive A web of adhesive that is backed with paper and used to fuse two pieces of fabric together.

*Ladder stitch An invisible stitch used to join together a seam opening on the right side of the fabric.

Miter A corner in which two pieces of fabric are brought together at a 45-degree angle. Most frequently used on fabric borders.

*Overcast stitch A hand stitch used to stitch the edges of fabric together. Also known as whip stitch or oversewing.

Pinking shears Scissors with serrated blades, used to prevent fabric edges from fraying.

Water-soluble vanishing fabric Fabric that disappears when immersed in water and rinsed.

Rotary cutter A wheel-type blade used for rapid and accurate cutting of fabric for patchwork.

*Running stitch A series of small, regular hand stitches gathered onto the needle as you stitch. Often used to gather fabric or for hand basting.

Selvage The edges of a length of fabric, which are woven so that the fabric threads cannot unravel.

*Slip stitch Small hand stitches used to join fabrics together invisibly. Useful for hemming.

Straight grain The grain of the fabric that runs parallel to either the warp or weft threads.

Straight stitch The standard stitch used in sewing machines that forms a straight line of stitches by drawing thread from the top of the machine (the spool of thread) through the needle and from the bottom (the bobbin) through the throat plate.

Template Paper, cardboard, or plastic pattern used as a guide for cutting fabric pieces to the same size and shape.

Tone The lightness or darkness of a color determined by the quantity of black in its makeup.

Warp The threads in a piece of fabric that have been stretched lengthwise in the loom. They run parallel to the selvages.

Weft The cross threads woven into the warp threads to make the fabric. They run perpendicular to the selvages.

Zigzag stitch A sewing machine stitch in which the needle swings from left to right to form a zigzagged line.

See pages 18 and 19 for how to work these hand stitches.

templates and patterns

These are the templates, the transfer, and the placement chart referred to in the project instructions in this book. There is a label alongside each illustration indicating the size at which it is shown. Where it is not shown at its actual size, or if you want to change the sizes, use a photocopier to enlarge or reduce it to the desired size.

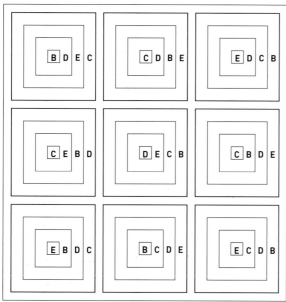

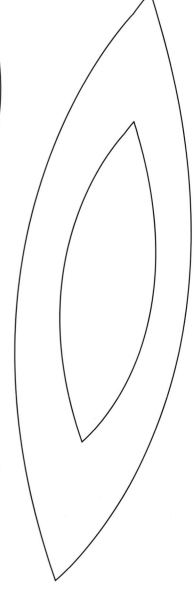

RAW APPLIQUÉ CUSHION (above)
See pages 44–47. Placement chart for colors of different appliqué patches.

fabric key
B = pomegranate SC09
C = chartreuse SC12
D = ginger SC01
E = sage SC17

APPLIQUÉ NAPKINS (above)
See pages 62–65. One appliqué petal and one appliqué flower center. Actual size shown.

APPLIQUÉ CUSHIONS (right)
See pages 78–83. Appliqué large petal for single-flower cushion. Appliqué small petal for four-flower cushion. Actual size shown.

TABLE RUNNER (right)
See pages 66–69. One large flower outline, with two smaller flower outlines inside. Actual size shown. Machine embroider flowers with one, two, or three lines of stitching, as preferred.

EMBROIDERED FLOWER (above)
See pages 56–61. Petal template (one of four identical petals). Actual size shown.

BUTTERFLY PICTURE (right)
See pages 40–43. Transfer shown at 50 percent of actual size. Enlarge 200 percent to achieve actual size.

fabric and thread information

The Kaffe Fassett fabrics used throughout this book are all from the Kaffe Fassett Collection by Rowan in 100 percent pure cotton. The width is approximately 45in (114cm).

All fabric should be washed before use to ensure that there is no uneven shrinkage or bleeding of colors in future washes. Press the fabric while it is still damp to return it to its natural crispness.

ABOUT THE KAFFE FASSETT COLLECTION FABRICS

These fabrics were all specially designed for patchworkers by Kaffe Fassett, one of the foremost colorists and most noted patchworkers of his day, and by select designers whose work he has chosen.

Kaffe's aim was to create a wide range of exciting designs that would complement each other across many of the patterns and colors, so the collection includes both plain fabrics (shot cottons), geometric designs (stripes and checks), and large bold patterns as well as small repeating patterns.

The Kaffe Fassett fabric collection grows each year, as a new design, usually in a series of half a dozen colors, is added, and some colors and patterns, inevitably, are dropped to make way for them. However, the collection has been designed with a unique color balance that works across many of the design ranges, so it should be easy to find substitute patterns and colors where necessary.

To order the Kaffe Fassett fabrics from the stockist nearest you, please contact the distributors at the addresses provided here (where there is not a distributor in a country, the nearest one is listed). The fabrics have names and color numbers to identify them; please use these when ordering fabrics. Resources for other fabric suppliers have also been included.

fabrics

Distributors for Rowan's Kaffe Fassett collection for USA and Canada

Westminster Fibers Inc.
4 Townsend West
Suite 8
Nashua, NH 03063
Tel: 603-886-5041
E-mail: rowan@westminsterfibers.com

Other fabric resources

Hancock Fabrics, Inc.
One Fashion Way
Baldwyn, MS 38824
Tel: 877-322-7427
www.hancockfabrics.com

Michael's Fabrics
4 Sandview Court
Baltimore, MD 21209
Tel: 877-266-8918

New England Fabrics
55 Ralston Street
Keene, NH 03431
Tel: 603-352-8683

sewing and embroidery threads

Coats & Clark
4135 South Stream Boulevard
Charlotte, NC 28217
Tel: 704-329-5016

Madeira
30 Bayside Court
Laconia, NH 03246
Tel: 800-225-3001

Sulky of America
P.O. Box 49412
Port Charlotte, FL 33949-4129
Tel: 800-874-4115
Fax: 941-743-4634
E-mail: info@sulky.com

Distributors for Rowan's Kaffe Fassett collection in other countries

AUSTRALIA
XLN Fabrics
2/21 Binney Road, Kings Park
NEW SOUTH WALES 2148
Tel: 61 2 96213066

BELGIUM
Rhinetex
Geurdeland 7
6673 DR ANDELST, HOLLAND
Tel: 31 488 480030

DENMARK
Industrial Textiles
Engholm Parkvej 1
DK 3450 ALLERØD
Tel: 45 48 17 20 55
E-mail: mail@indutex.dk

FINLAND
Coats Opti OY
Ketjutie 3
04220 KERAVA
Tel: 358 9 274 871
E-mail: coatsoptisales@coats.com

FRANCE
Rhinetex, Geurdeland 7
6673 DR ANDELST, HOLLAND
Tel: 31 488 480030

GERMANY
Rhinetex
Geurdeland 7
6673 DR ANDELST, HOLLAND
Tel: 31 488 480030

HOLLAND
Rhinetex
Geurdeland 7
6673 DR ANDELST
Tel: 31 488 480030

ICELAND
Storkurinn
Laugavegi 59
101 REYKJAVIK
Tel: 354 551 8258
E-mail: malin@mmedia.is

ITALY
DL SRL
Via Piave 24-26
20016 PERO
MILANO
Tel: 39 02 339 10 180

JAPAN
Yokota & Co. Ltd.
5-14 2 Chome Minamikyuhoojimachi
Chuo-Ku
OSAKA
Tel: 81 6 6251 7179

NEW ZEALAND
Fabco Limited
P.O. Box 84-002
Westgate
AUCKLAND 1250
Tel: 64 9 411 9996

NORWAY
Industrial Textiles
Engholm Parkvej 1
DK 3450 ALLERØD
DENMARK
Tel: 45 48 17 20 55
E-mail: mail@indutex.dk

SOUTH KOREA
Coats Korea Co. Ltd.
5F Kuckdong B/D
935-40 Bangbae-Dong
Seocho-Gu
SEOUL
Tel: (82) 2 521 6262
Fax: (82) 2 521 5181

SOUTH AFRICA
Arthur Bales PTY Ltd.
PO Box 44644
LINDEN 2104
Tel: 27 11 888 2401
E-mail: arthurb@new.co.za

SPAIN
Lucretia Beleta Patchwork
Dr Rizal 12
08006 BARCELONA
Tel: 34 93 41 59555

SWITZERLAND
Rhinetex
Geurdeland 7
6673 DR ANDELST
HOLLAND
Tel: 31 488 480030

SWEDEN
Industrial Textiles
Engholm Parkvej 1
DK 3450 ALLERØD
DENMARK
Tel: 45 48 17 20 55
E-mail: mail@indutex.dk

TAIWAN
Long Teh Trading Co.
3F No 19–2
Kung Yuan Road
TAICHUNG
Tel: 886 4 2225 6698

UK
Rowan Yarns
Green Lane Mill
Holmfirth
West Yorkshire
HD9 2DX
ENGLAND
E-mail: mail@knitrowan.com

index

acknowledgments

AUTHOR'S ACKNOWLEDGMENTS

I would like to thank Susan, John, Carrie, and Anne for making this book happen! To my sister Kate for spending her weekends helping me, hand stitching the projects and being wonderful. Thanks to my parents for all their love, support, and delicious meals-on-wheels service! Finally, thanks to all my friends for being amazing, especially Jez for turning up at exactly the right time and making me laugh!

PUBLISHERS' ACKNOWLEDGMENTS

The publishers would like to thank Anne Wilson for her design, John Heseltine for his photography, Carrie Hill for her artworks, Sally Harding for her editorial work, Pauline Smith for her technical advice, Ann Hinchcliffe for her support, and Marie Lorimer for the index.